The
ACADEMIC
BESTIARY

The ACADEMIC BESTIARY

by Richard Armour

Illustrated by Paul Darrow

William Morrow & Company, Inc., New York, 1974

Printed in the United States of America.

1 2 3 4 5 79 78 77 76 75

Library of Congress Cataloging in Publication Data

Armour, Richard Willard (date)
   The academic bestiary.

   1. Universities and colleges—United States. 2. Universities and colleges—Anecdotes facetiae, satire, etc. I. Title.
LA227.3.A75   378′.002′07   74-16011
ISBN 0-688-02884-5

Design by Helen Roberts

Dedicated
to any friends I may still have left
in Academe

The Strange Land of Academe

UNLIKE Samuel Butler's Erewhon, which is Nowhere spelled backward, there is nothing backward about Academe. Indeed many of Conservative Bent think Academe too forward, as well as out of touch with Reality. If there were another name for Academe it might be Erehwemos, which has a scholarly Greek sound.*

Thus, though Academe may seem fanciful and fantastic, it really exists and is neither so perfect nor so inaccessible as Erewhon or Shangri-La or Plato's Republic or the land of the Houyhnhnms. Sometimes it is about as far out of town as Walden or Brook Farm, but often it is adjacent to or even in the center of a metropolis. Nonetheless, though it is easily reached it is not easily breached.

* Spelled backward, as you have probably noticed, it is Somewhere. It is also more accurate than Butler's spelling of Erewhon, which should have been Erehwon.

It is one thing to be a Casual Visitor, but quite another to become an accepted member of the community, a full-fledged or even half-fledged Academian.

One of the many strange things about Academe is that physically it can be so close to the Real World and yet spiritually and psychologically so completely out of it, often failing to understand it and sometimes bitterly antagonistic toward it. Most Academians come from the Real World or the Outside World, and some eventually return to it. Before they enter Academe they have human characteristics, but these they soon lose, in the process of adaptation, and become the grotesque creatures which will be described in the pages that follow.

Wherever Academe is, the route to it is much the same. For the Student it is through the Elementary School, Junior High School, and High School. Of course the Student may take the less traveled and more expensive by-way, or buyway, that leads through the Private School, confusingly known in the Old Country as the Public School. Such an institution, especially the Prestigious Private School, may give a foretaste of Academe, but still a foretaste is not quite the same as the entire meal.

During all of this Schooling the Student assumes few if any of the characteristics of the denizens of Academe. It may therefore enter Academe quite innocently, with a virgin mind if nothing else, lured into it by Status-Seeking, pressure from its Peer Group, or Family Pride. In time of war it may be seeking refuge from that fearsome ogre, the Draft. Sometimes it knows even before it enters Academe that it does not belong there. Sometimes it discovers this only after it is inside, but, even after seeing through it, it stubbornly or docilely sees it through. Sometimes it leaves abruptly when faced by one or more of those three frightful Fates: Failure, Suspension, and Expulsion.

For the Professor or the Administrator the route is the same but longer, including the ultimate transmogrification of Graduate School. The Academian of this species will have surmounted such awesome barriers as the Dissertation and the Oral. It is such an Academian, unlike the Student, that becomes wholly identified with Academe and gives its heart and soul to it. Some, to be sure, do not believe in the soul, while others are thought by Students to be heartless.*

Life in Academe is different from life in the Real World in many ways, some of them incredible to the inexperienced. For instance there are only nine months in the Academic Year, and the Calendar besides being full of dates is full of Events. Commencement is when the Academic Year finishes instead of when it commences. Everyone carries a Load, either a Teaching Load or a Course Load, but the Load is invisible except for the anguished look on the face of an Academian that thinks itself overloaded. Though many Liberal Academians believe in a Classless Society, there is no place where there are more classes, the lowest being the Eight o'Clock Class. And so it goes, though one wonders how.

Academe is not a Never-Never Land, it is an Ever-Ever Land. There is no doubt that, unbelievable as it is, it exists and has existed for hundreds of years. Some trace it as far back as Socrates (469–399 B.C.), who was accused of corrupting the young by exposing them to Knowledge. If Socrates seemed not reluctant to drink the hemlock, it may be because he realized what he had created: the *genus Academicum*.

---

* A dull Professor may even be considered lifeless, or at any rate far from lively.

The Activist

(Tempori parendum) *

THE Activist is the activest of the Students, actively trying
to find itself by asking searching questions and looking
into anything that bears looking into.† This may lead to
what the Resident Psychiatrist calls an Identity Crisis. If
the Activist finally manages to find itself and discovers it
is in Academe and doing none too well academically, it
may ask, "Why am I here?" As Professors often say, "That
is a Good Question." ‡

Then again the Activist may be opposed to the Establishment, perhaps because it had no part in establishing
it. It may also believe that male and female Students

* We must move with the times. The Activist is therefore identified with
Movements, no matter in what direction or under whose direction.

† Except a mirror.

‡ Better than most answers to it.

4

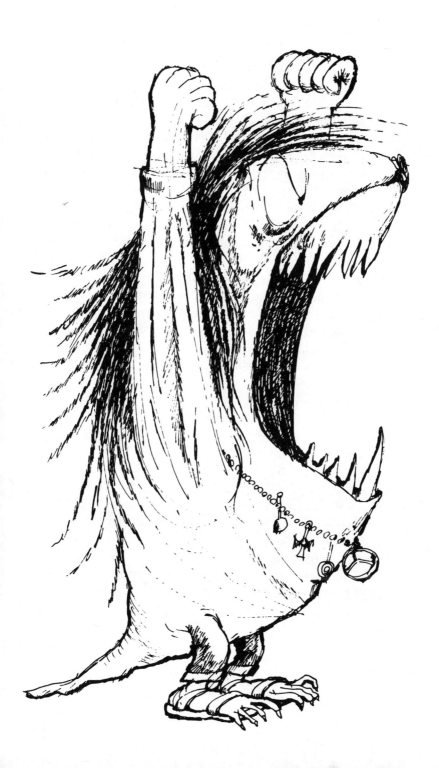

should look upon each other as brothers and sisters, especially if it is an only child and does not know how unpleasant this can be.

The Activist is concerned about Apathy and, still worse, those apathetic about Apathy. Such Students, it thinks, have the wrong lifestyle, as well as hairstyle, paying more attention to Professors than to Protestors. As the Activist says, they are not "with it," which must mean they are without it. The Activist tells apathetic Students to "do their thing," without saying what their thing is or what to do with it.

To achieve its ends, the Activist usually runs for Student Body President, Editor of the Campus Paper, or Chairman of the Student Council. It models its campaigns on those of politicians in the Outside World, though it has already learned most of what it needs to know in the classroom, including how to have term papers ghostwritten. If not elected, it may threaten to go to the Ombudsman, a terrifying prospect.

The Activist wishes to bring Equality, Relevance, Innovation, and Meaningfulness into Academe, even at the risk of overcrowding. It would right wrongs by giving more voice in Administration to the Student that has grown hoarse from shouting.* Thanks to the Activist, Students are on Faculty and Trustee Committees, thus compensating for the stupidity and hypocrisy of any behind-the-times Member that still believes in Marriage and the Capitalistic System.

The remarkable thing about the Activist is that, despite all of its activities, it is usually able to graduate. It then goes out into the Real World and gradually calms down or deactivates.

---

* Especially shouting down speakers having a different Point of View.

The Admission

(Aestimatis capitis) *

ALSO known as the Dean of Admissions and the Director of Admissions, the Admission is always out looking, or scouting. It is constantly On the Road. What it is looking for is high SAT's, high Grades, Athletes, Student Leaders, and children of wealthy parents. It looks high and low, but prefers to look high. Whenever it meets a creature that looks promising for Academe, the first question it asks is "How did you do on your Boards?"

This is only one of many questions asked by the Admission during the ordeal known as the Interview. Acting at one moment like a guard dog and the next like a shepherd, the Admission makes it look hard to get in if it is easy and easy to get in if it is hard. By the time it asks its final

---

* Estimation of the head. In admitting an Athlete, however, it may be estimation of the biceps, triceps, pectoral muscles, and weight stripped.

question, "Have you any more questions?" (the Applicant not as yet having had a chance to ask a question), the Applicant is too distraught psychologically to apply to any other part of Academe, which is what the Admission intended.

The Admission has a bright, optimistic look on its face, hoping to convince the Prospective Applicant, or Prospect, that Academe, and especially its part of Academe, is perfect, or slightly better than perfect. It is only when, late in the season, it has to descend the ladder taking it down among the Alternates * that it assumes a gloomy, even frightened expression. The Alternate may have a low Verbal, which is not only unattractive but inclined to drag, and it may also require a Scholarship. An Applicant that is both stupid and unable to pay its own way is known as a Last Resort and is used to fill an empty Dorm room. Besides, who knows? It may have Hidden Capabilities.

In its search for Prospects, the Admission leaves no stone unturned. Its assistant, the Field Representative, points out the most promising stones and helps turn them.

In a Good Year, the Admission admits mostly Applicants in the Upper Percentile, which it reaches with some difficulty, often picking its way upward like a Mountain Goat. In a Bad Year, however, it may admit anything.† It puts most of the blame on the Declining Birth Rate, which helps the unemployment situation except for that of Directors of Admission.

The Admission must find standing important, even when sitting, because of its constant reference to Freshman Standing, Advanced Standing, and the like. "Let's all pull together," it says, even when what it needs is a little push.

The Admission reports to the President and to the Trustees, usually giving a Glowing Report or painting a Rosy Picture. Such a painting may be a little surrealistic or unrealistic. If the colors run, so does the Admission, seeking out a part of Academe where its work is unknown and it can make a Fresh Start.

---

* And, even lower, to the Illiterates.

† Anything, that is, but an error on its own part. "What went wrong?" it asks, rather than "What did I do wrong?" or "What did I fail to do right?"

The Alum

(Saepe creat melles aspera spina rosas) *

FEW creatures in Academe have so many names as the Alum. The Alum is also known as the Alumnus (male), the Alumna (female), the Alumni (more than one male or male and female Alum), and the Alumnae (more than one female Alum).† It is also sometimes called an Old Grad but rarely (within hearing, which must be quite close) a Very Old Grad or a Senile Old Grad, the acronym for which is SOG.

When it is On Campus for a Reunion, arranged by the

---

* The sharp thorn often produces soft roses. However the Alum, which may have taken some sharp thrusts from Professors and others while in Academe, does not necessarily turn soft in Later Life. If it becomes an Executive, those who serve under it may think it has developed not into a rose but into a cactus.

† Unlike the chemical alum, the Alum is pronounced on its second syllable and may be a pronounced success in the Outside World.

Alumni Secretary in concert with the Director of Development, a concert to which tax-deductible tickets are sold for the benefit of the Scholarship Fund or the renovation of Old Main, the Alum behaves in a curious way. If it is an Alumnus it gives another Alumnus, especially if it is a Classmate,* a bear hug and a slap on the back. Neither of these does any damage unless the Alum being grappled with has arthritis. If it is an Alumna it gives another Alumna a warm embrace and a kiss, the embrace being to see whether the Alumna's figure is for real. Sometimes an Alumnus and an Alumna, not noticing the difference in their endings, get mixed up about this.

The Alum grows misty-eyed when it refers to its Alma Mater, which apparently is as important to it as its Dura Mater, a tough, fibrous membrane, lined with endothelium, which envelops the brain. The Alma Mater develops not so much the Alum's brain as its heart. That is probably why the Alum says such things as "My Alma

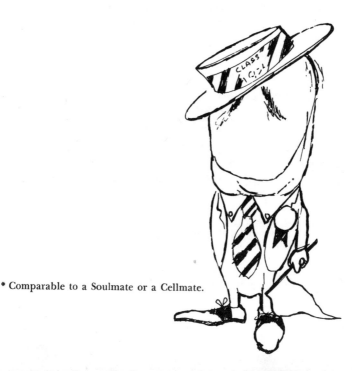

* Comparable to a Soulmate or a Cellmate.

Mater tugs at my heartstrings." However, the heartstrings of the Alum seem to be attached not to its heart but to its tear ducts.

One thing the Alum deplores is Change, which it thinks deplorable. It may itself have changed, and times may have changed, but it expects its Alma Mater to remain as it was in the Good Old Days. Those were the days when Students respected Professors and believed what they said, especially when they said the same things year after year, indicating that what they said was Worth Repeating. Those were also the days when there was an Honor Code, which forbade any Student to get caught cheating.

When, after a Reunion, an Alum returns to the Outside World, it becomes preoccupied with other matters, such as Making a Living, and its Alma Mater fades into the background. However, memories are awakened when the *Newsletter* arrives. This it scans carefully, to see (1) whether its name is mentioned and (2) who has died. It is not pleased if its name turns up in the latter list.

All too frequently an Appeal * is received on behalf of the Alumni Fund. Momentarily the Alum is Turned Off. "All they want of me is my money," it says, and for once it is right. But usually it gives until it hurts, the pain coming quickly and being felt in the region of the wallet.

Though briefly distressed when the Changes become too great, the Activists become too active, and the Administration becomes too passive, the Alum remains loyal. A disloyal Alum is beneath notice.†

---

* Or a Call for Help, also known as a Dun. It is repeatedly pointed out that the Alum paid for only a small part of its Education and all its life will be indebted to the Endowment.

† And should therefore be relegated to a footnote, or, if there were any such thing, an underfoot note.

The Anthropologist

(Homo mensura) *

THE Anthropologist closely resembles the Sociologist, both being of the genus Social Scientist. Rather than studying Society, the Anthropologist focuses on Man, which it finds fascinating and baffling.† When the Anthropologist is in Deep Study, a subterranean place where it ruminates, cogitates, ratiocinates, deliberates, and estivates, ‡ it may also be engaged in examining the skeleton of Prehistoric Man. Usually, however, it leaves the bones of Early Man to the Paleontologist, preferring flesh, blood, skin, and what in the Renaissance was known as the Whole Man. §

---

* Man is the measure. Consider, for example, the foot.

† Also Woman, which is even more so.

‡ Passes the summer in a Torpor, which is more comfortable than a Land Rover.

§ Early Man is inclined to be more holey, at least by the time he is dug up.

Like the Paleontologist, it is interested in finding out whether Man evolved from the Ape or the Ape evolved from Man. Since this is difficult to determine, it spends most of its time traveling around to get a close look at Primitive Tribes, trying to figure out how they are able to exist without the automobile, air conditioning, and television commercials. The Anthropologist usually travels on a Grant, either a Government Grant or a Foundation Grant. Even when it is in a Deep Study it may be on a Grant, depending on it not only for transportation but for sustenance.

The Anthropologist has no distinguishing feature except its nose, which it is always sticking into things, especially anything connected with Man. While the Anthropologist is greatly interested in Man, Man has very little interest in the Anthropologist. There are those who think the Anthropologist is actually an Ant-hropologist, or Ant that is forever hropping around and is up to no good.

Preoccupied by its study of Man, and of itself, the Anthropologist, like other denizens of Academe, in time becomes afflicted by Specialization.* It may then take on the characteristics of the Anthropogenist, the Anthroponomist, or even the Anthropoclimatologist. If it begins to look hungrily at Man, this may indicate it is toying with the idea of becoming an Anthropophagist. The more technical term for the Anthropophagist, also known as the Anthropophagite, is of course the Cannibal. However, statistics show that more Anthropologists are eaten by Cannibals than Cannibals are eaten by Anthropologists. If the Anthropologist's mouth is wide open it is more likely because of amazement than hunger.

---

* There is nothing special about Specialization. Only through Specialization can a Professor get to know so much about so little as eventually to achieve the Academian's goal of knowing everything about nothing worth knowing anything about.

The Apple Polisher

(Nulla fides fronti) *

UNLESS the seating is alphabetical and its name begins
with some letter other than *A* or *B,* the Apple Polisher
sits on the front row. It is not that its hearing is poor but
that it wishes to see and, above all, to be seen. In fact it
wishes to be seen so closely that each expression of interest, understanding, and adulation will be observed by
the Professor.

The Apple Polisher does not actually polish apples.
This is what is known in Academe as a Figure of Speech.
The Apple Polisher may have given polished apples to
the teacher in High School, but now it brings other gifts.
If a male, it may bring nothing but an attentive, admiring
look, meanwhile cocking an ear † so as not to miss a word

---

* No trust in the countenance. I.e., looks can be deceiving (and so also
can words).

† Unlike a pistol, an ear makes no distracting click when it is cocked.

of the Professor's lecture, even while thinking of something else. If it is a female, it depends less on the ear than on other parts of the anatomy.

The Apple Polisher is inclined to fawn. If it were a real fawn it would rub its soft fur against the Professor's leg and lick the Professor's hand, meanwhile looking up endearingly with its soft brown eyes. Its purpose is to make the Professor look upon it with tenderness and affection, as well as to inflate the Professor's ego, even though it is already inflated almost to the bursting point. Only in this way can the Apple Polisher get a grade of A or B instead of the C or D it deserves.

Occasionally a Professor is aware of the intentions of the Apple Polisher and tries to lecture to the Average Students in the middle rows and the Somnolent Students in the back row. It may have its attention called to the front row from time to time, however, if the female Student with what is known as Cleavage drops its pencil. When it stoops to pick it up, the Professor, despite a Supreme Effort of Will, drops its eyes. No matter how tired its eyes are from reading papers and examinations, they rise, or lower, to the occasion.*

What the Apple Polisher fails to realize is that it is in Academe not to polish anything but to acquire polish. That, however, is a Subtle Distinction, better left to the Philologists and the Philosophers.

* As a consequence the Professor may think better (and more often) of the Student.

The Artist

(Ars est celare artem) *

THE Artist may be a Painter, a Sculptor, a Ceramicist, or a Weaver.† No matter what its species within the genus, it has the common element of Creativity. That is, it creates something out of nothing or, about as often, nothing out of something. If it is a Painter, it may paint either oils or watercolors, and this is not easy, despite the help of an easel.

When the Painter shows Students how to paint nudes, the Students in Elementary Painting can at first do nothing but stare at the Model, which is getting paid by the hour and has no reason to complain unless the Art Studio is too cool.‡ In Advanced Painting the Students have ad-

* Art lies in the concealment of art. Some Artists, especially the Moderns, are highly successful at this.

† Especially if it drinks a little too much.

‡ Body heat, with enough Students painting feverishly, usually keeps the room comfortably warm.

vanced considerably, for one thing believing there is nothing nudesworthy about nudes. Nor do such Students have trouble mixing paints.* In fact the Student may by this time prefer to paint Still Lifes, such as a bowl of fruit or a pair of old shoes. Whatever it paints, it should follow the Cardinal Principle that the picture must in no way resemble the object it is depicting. Otherwise there would be nothing left for the Art Critic to figure out.

Another type of Artist, the Sculptor, may model a Model in clay and then have it cast in bronze.† Or the Sculptor may use a mallet and chisel, whacking away at a piece of granite or marble and breaking it into smaller and smaller pieces. Sometimes the chisel slips and a design is made that the Sculptor had not intended. In the finished work, this is called an Inspiration and the Sculptor is hailed as a Genius.

Students watch, fascinated, while the Sculptor works, hoping against hope, and sometimes for hope, that the Sculptor will miss the chisel, hammering a thumb into pulp or causing a commissioned statue ‡ to split right down the middle with what was intended to be the final blow.

The Ceramicist works in clay and therefore is a mess at the end of the day's classes when it emerges. Most of the time it is throwing pots, which the Students must learn to catch if they wish to survive the course, or even survive. Once a pot has been properly thrown it is placed in a kiln § and cooked until it is done. "Well done," in fact the Ceramicist may say approvingly.

Should the Artist be a Weaver, it works at a loom. A

* Getting their paints mixed up with the paints of others.
† And as far away as possible.
‡ There are no noncommissioned statues, though some include the privates. Most of these are for private collections, with fig leaves extra.
§ Pronounced "kill" by those who know what goes on inside.

Japanese Weaver may say, "Meet me at Loom 405," when there is no such loom number. But it is not necessary to be Japanese to become confused about which is the warp and which is the woof. The warp does not distort the loom, nor does the woof bite the weaver at work. On a loom beautifully designed textiles and tapestries are woven that may be used as rugs or hung in a gallery.*

The Artist is artfully artless about its appearance, trying hard to appear casual about its attire. All of its talents must go into painting, sculpture, ceramics, or whatever. "Throw yourself into your work," the Artist tells its Students, watching approvingly while they plunge headlong into canvases and even blocks of marble.†

Aware that there are many Schools of Criticism, the Artist says, "Beauty is in the eye of the beholder." Then it refers the beholder to an ophthalmologist for removal of the foreign object. For the most part the Artist is content to receive a salary from teaching, augmented by the sale of its works to Patrons of the Arts, people who fill their homes with Originals. What is impressive about an Original is not so much its originality as the price tag, which is slightly larger than the name of the Artist.

Ars gratia artis, or "Art for the sake of artists," is the Latin way of putting it. More sympathetic are the French, with their *L'art pour l'art,* or "Art, poor art." But if art is poor, there is no one to blame but the Artist. This is also true if the Artist is poor, though the Artist may say the fault lies with those who may not know art but know what they like, which is probably limited to the works of the famous German artist Kitsch.

* This last, however, is the Artist's macabre ambition.
† In the latter case they may plunge in headlong but emerge headshort.

The Athlete

(Genus musculum)

THE Athlete * is probably the largest, strongest creature in Academe. It is so heavy it has to be supported by an Athletic Scholarship, which is not to be confused with an Athletic Supporter.

Everything about the Athlete is athletic. It has, for instance, not only Athlete's Foot but Athlete's Head, the latter not helped by any powder or lotion. It also has enormous muscles it flexes from time to time, partly to develop them further and partly to impress those creatures of Academe, such as the Grind and the Phi Bete, which have no observable musculature.

The Athlete may be either male or female. However, the male Athlete has more appeal to the average female

* Often pronounced "Athalete" by those who find it hard to say "thl." The medical term *thlipsis* is difficult even for an M.D.

than the female Athlete has to the average male. The male Athlete is much admired for its hairy chest. No matter what athletic costume it may wear, it tries to leave an opening so that some of this hair will show.

Some believe the Athlete is out of place in Academe and belongs in the Animal Kingdom. This is perhaps because of its resemblance to such animals as the Bear and the

Gorilla, both being muscular and hairy. It is sometimes asked, "What brought the Athlete to Academe?" The answer is that it was probably the Admission or the Coach that sought out the Athlete and waved an Athletic Scholarship under its nose. Though protected by a nose guard, the Athlete caught the scent and lost consciousness. Upon awakening it found itself in Academe, among such strange creatures as the Intellectual and the Brain.

Unlike the Bear, the Athlete hibernates at odd times, sleeping through the months when it is Out of Season and nothing is expected of it. Then the other Students of Academe, busy studying, are hardly aware of its existence. Being In Season is, to the Athlete, comparable to being In Heat in the Animal Kingdom.

Nonetheless the Athlete is of a charitable nature and makes its contribution to School Spirit and the All-Around image. Without the Athlete, Academe would not be the same.* Also that endangered species, the Cheerleader, might become extinct.

The Athlete is especially meaningful to the Old Grad, notably the one that can remember nothing from four years in Academe but the scores in the annual Big Game.

In fairness, it should be remarked that there is nothing to keep the Athlete from becoming a Good Student or even a Rhodes Scholar. In fact the Athlete has a better chance to become the latter than most creatures in Academe.† Moreover, after Graduation the Athlete may become a Success, having learned in Academe, if it learned nothing else, that it is not the way you play the game that counts, it is winning.

---

* We are not saying whether better or worse.

† "Have you ever rowed?" the Selection Committee may ask. Some think the name should be changed to Rowed Scholarship, since the emphasis is as much on the scull as on the skull.

The Campus

(Ubi mel, ibi apes) *

WHILE most of Academe is Cultural, the Campus is largely Horticultural, and instead of moving about it is moved about on. Almost everything in Academe, as a matter of fact, is either On Campus or Off Campus, which is an Important Distinction. Certain things can be done Off Campus, for instance, which would be Grounds for Expulsion if done On Campus. As it is, enough is done On Campus to cause the Campus to be concerned for its Reputation.

The Campus is divided into two parts, Buildings and Grounds (the latter only occasionally having any relationship to Grounds for Expulsion, referred to above). The two parts are held together by green tendrils and ivylike leaves arising from the earthy portion of the Campus. This

---

* Where the honey is, there are the bees. That may be why the Campus is usually abuzz.

is probably why the Campus is known by some, such as the Nostalgic Alum, for its Halls of Ivy, though others are more inclined to call attention to its Ivory Tower, where it does its thinking, undisturbed by Reality.

The heart of the Campus * is a rectangular space known as the Quad. It is green, and usually dotted with Students. Occasionally a dot will turn into a dash, as a Student hurries off to a class. Mostly, however, pairs of Students remain motionless, or almost motionless, all over the Campus. Though they walk on the Campus, sit on the Campus, and lie on the Campus, the Campus does not protest, though Students sometimes do. That is when the Campus, which is normally restful, is in a state of Unrest.

Here and there on the Campus may be seen the name of a Donor. How and why these names got there is puzzling to those not familiar with the work of the Development, whose motto is "Where there's a Will, there's a way." † But for the Donor, many parts of the Campus would be undeveloped and unproductive, perhaps a barren waste.

Grotesque as the Campus is, it is dearly loved by the Old Grad who returns to it at certain times, known as Reunions. He may even shed a tear, when he thinks of how much more beautiful the Campus was in His Day, and this helps keep the Campus green, especially when it is accompanied by a Class Gift. If he graduated in the first class, it may be a First-Class Gift. The Campus may not benefit from it, however, unless it is specifically specified.‡

* Any ticking sound might, during a Demonstration, be not the heart but a bomb.

† Lawyers also have their motto, however, which is "Where there's a Will, there's a way out."

‡ An Unrestricted Gift, which is what the Administration prefers, can be used for anything essential, such as a new car for the President.

The Classicist

(Ζωή μου, σᾶς ἀγαπῶ)*

To the Classicist, the Good Old Days were about 500 B.C.†
That was when what are called Dead Languages were still
alive. One curious thing that appeals to the Classicist is
that people in those days lived backward, Sophocles for
example having been born in 496 and having died in 406.
Actually he was born not in 496 but in "496?" ‡

The Classicist may specialize in Ancient Greece or in

* Usually translated "My life, I love thee," and used as a refrain in
Byron's "Maid of Athens, Ere We Part." But since Byron refrained from
very little, when it came to women, and had a girl in every town, including Athens, it more likely means, "Zoë mine, I love thee."

† Before Colleges.

‡ With some of the Classical writers it is apparently questionable not
only when they were born but whether. Take Homer, for instance. He is
said to have "flourished about the ninth century B.C." There is no reference to whether he was ever born or, for that matter, ever died.

Ancient Rome. One thing all Classicists have in common is a love of the Ancient. Another is a love of Beauty and Truth. If, as Keats wrote, "Beauty is truth, truth beauty," and also "That is all ye need to know," the Classicist should find it simple to teach Students the Fundamentals of Classicism, one of the fundamentals of which is simplicity. Professors of Greek or Latin with young girls in their classes would not appear to be exclusively in love with the Ancient. In fact some might wish to alter the lines in Keats's "Ode on a Grecian Urn" ever so slightly, to make them "Beauty is youth, youth beauty. . . . That is all ye need, ye know."

The Classicist lives in the past but also in the present, and therefore may be said to lead two lives. However, it is able to get only one life insured, most life-insurance agents thinking *hubris* an incurable disease. The Classicist whose interest is Ancient Greece often speaks of "the gory of Greece," probably having in mind the Peloponnesian War and the battles with the Persians, Macedonians, Romans, and others. It is a little embarrassing to the Classicist that, for all their love of the gods, the Greeks were actually Hellenes.*

A specialty of the Classicist is, of course, the Greek tongue, which was covered with all sorts of strange accent marks that must have made it difficult for the taste buds.

As for the Classicist that specializes in Ancient Rome, it knows all about such things as the Colosseum, where large crowds gathered to watch Christians thrown to the Lions; † the Catacombs, which were not, as you might suppose, places where they combed cats; the Temple of the Vestal Virgins, which was quite a contrast to the Public Baths; and the Orgies, where Romans indulged in sex while being fed grapes.

Rome had both big wars and Punic Wars. It also had what it called *Panem et circenses,* or free bread and shows at circuses, a predecessor of the Welfare State.

As the Classicist knows, great deeds were accomplished by Julius Caesar, such as dividing Gaul into three parts. Nevertheless he was murdered in the Senate, where Senators not only looked daggers at one another but used them.

Then came the Decline and Fall. The thought of it brings tears to the eyes of the Classicist. "Those gruesome Goths! Those vulgar Vandals!" it can be heard to mutter. It realizes, however, that but for the Decline and Fall few would ever have heard of Edward Gibbon.‡

---

* Some of the Greek gods or demigods were half animal and half man, and one must look closely to see which half is which. Satyrs had the tail and ears of a horse and were the ancient counterpart of the modern Lecher, which is excessively human all over.

† This was long before the Rotarians and the Kiwanians. Homer, by the way, had nothing to do with the origin of baseball. However, Colosseum fans, with their signals of thumb up or thumb down, may have given the idea to the modern umpire.

‡ Or, to put it another way, Gibbon would have been short six volumes.

The Coach

(Qualis rex, talis grex) *

THE Coach is usually given a nickname by the Athletes. It is something affectionate but descriptive, such as "Bear" or "Bull" or "Pappy." The Coach itself was once an Athlete, as it is not averse to telling the Athletes, and therefore understands them, which is difficult for some of their Professors.†

The Coach coaches, which is a physical form of teaching. Instead of using a textbook the Coach uses Experience and Example. It may have forgotten it is no longer an Athlete and that in changing from an Athlete to a Coach it has grown larger in the middle, while its Throwing Arm

---

* As the shepherd, so the flock. There is nothing sheepish, however, about the Coach.

† Athletes may find it even more difficult to understand these same Professors.

has become weaker. It breathes heavily, which at least is better than drinking heavily, and may learn, before it does itself any permanent harm, not to Demonstrate but to Describe and Explain. Though it becomes winded when it runs, it merely becomes windy when it Explains.* Since it finds it increasingly difficult to do some of the things it wishes the Athletes to do, it may helpfully suggest, "Don't do as I do, do as I say."

Even more than the Athlete, the Coach's goal, which is marked by goalposts, is to Win. Most of all it wants a Winning Season or, the pinnacle of achievement, a Championship. Any of these would make it possible for the Coach to keep its job or to find a Coaching Position† elsewhere in Academe that would pay what it considers a Living Wage, in other words about as much as is paid to a Full Professor or a Dean.‡

The Coach is known for its pithy, aphoristic remarks, such as "Get in there and fight" and "Give it all you've got." It will be noticed that none of these employs a word of more than one syllable. Since it probably did not major in English, the Coach is not concerned about being monosyllabic.§ What it worries about is having an Athlete come down with mononucleosis just before the Big Game.

Mostly the Coach will be found sitting on the Bench or pacing forth and back. From time to time it shouts obscenities at the Referee. This it does as loudly as it can without being loud enough for the Referee to hear. The

---

* If it is called "Bull" rather than "Bear" it may be because of some remark made by an Academian that chanced to be listening.

† Standing, sitting, prone, or supine, depending on what the Coach is demonstrating.

‡ If the Coach has a long string of Championships it may be paid as much as the President, and sometimes more.

§ An exception is the Debate Coach, which lives by the motto "Words, not deeds."

Coach pretends not to be nervous, even while pulling hunks of hair out of its head or chewing a handful of small stones it mistakenly grabbed up instead of antacid tablets.

At the end of a Winning Season the Coach may be given an Automobile. At the end of a Losing Season the Coach may be given the Gate. As the Administration says tersely, "We need New Blood. And we need a Coach with Guts." Apparently the old Coach swallowed too many of those small stones it was chewing on.

The Co-Ed

(Bellatrix) *

THE Co-Ed is of the *genus Studens* but is a species that consists solely of females. It is perhaps the only creature in Academe that is hyphenated, something that happens to it just as it enters Academe.† One result of this is its division into two parts, the Co and the Ed, both of which are designed to attract the male, or *masculus,* without which the Co-Ed could not exist.

There is a sinuous, serpentine quality about the Co-Ed, particularly when observed from the rear as it moves from place to place. The males of all species in Academe, even and especially the older Professors, are fascinated by every movement of the Co-Ed, whether front or rear. The Co-Ed

* A female warrior. The Co-Ed, though not actually a warrior, may have to fight off male students.

† During the secret, primitive rites of Matriculation.

is noteworthy for its curves, which have to be seen to be believed.* These vary from Co-Ed to Co-Ed, in extent though not in location.

One feature of the Co-Ed should not be overlooked. That is its sharp tongue. Except when used to make cutting remarks, however, it is not visible. Most of the time it keeps its tongue in its cheek, where it can do no harm.

It might be thought that the Co-Ed would live in a Co-Ed Dorm, and it sometimes does. Often, however, it lives in a Single-Sex Dorm, usually † in a Dorm with those of the same sex. Its Sex Drive may, however, drive it elsewhere from time to time. The Co-Ed may even live Off Campus, spending only its days On Campus. If such is the case, where and how it spends its nights is a Personal Matter.

The Co-Ed is usually a Good Student, or better than most male Students in Academe, these being too busy studying the Co-Ed to study anything else. The curvaceous Co-Ed, undulating from the Classroom to the Library, is a Distraction. Yet the Co-Ed is not only intensely but highly regarded and is sometimes known as a Brain. This is a part of the Co-Ed that does not show, except in the Classroom. Also the Co-Ed is envied by the male Student because it finds it easier to get into that part of Academe known as the Graduate School, especially the Prestigious Graduate School. This was not always true but is a Recent Development.‡

---

* Some, that is, are to be believed, while others are believed to have been falsified.

† I.e., most of the time.

‡ Partly a result of the Women's Liberation Movement, a movement quite unlike the sinuous movement mentioned above.

The Commencement

(Finis et de novo)

THE Commencement is a strange creature, which makes it quite at home in Academe. It emerges only once a year, in the spring. Academians, as well as those from the Outside World, gather to catch a glimpse of it before it vanishes from sight after this single but dramatic appearance.*

It is a colorful species, covered with Academic Regalia, which include a robe, a hood, and a mortarboard. The hood could be placed over its head, in event of a sudden downpour, but is usually worn casually around its neck. The mortarboard is not really a board covered with mortar or cement but a cap with a square top from which a tassel dangles in the Commencement's eye. It is probably as

---

* Some compare it to the groundhog but notice that, in the strange light of Academe, it is cast by its shadow.

ridiculous and impractical a type of headgear as can be found, but is highly prized in Academe, especially when the tassel is moved from the right side of the mortarboard to the left, in a ceremony comparable to puberty rites.*

The first part of the Commencement is the Academic Procession, headed by a Professor with a Mace. The Mace is a wicked-looking staff or club with spikes at one end and is intended to help the Professor, known as the Marshal, to keep everyone in line and if possible (though this is rarely achieved) in step. Though the Marshal may be a Professor of Philosophy known On Campus as a Radical Thinker and even a member of the ACLU, for the moment it is the embodiment of Tradition and Law and Order. It could be that pride in office and in academic panoply briefly overcomes its distaste for the Establishment.

By far the longest part of the Commencement is the Commencement Address. It is difficult for the Commencement Speaker (1) to live up to the introduction by the President † and (2) to crowd into forty minutes all the truisms, clichés, and oft-heard exhortations that are anticipated by the audience. The Commencement Speaker is frequently interrupted by applause, especially at those times when it seems to have said everything that could possibly be said and therefore to have concluded.‡

Sometimes the Commencement Speaker is given an Honorary Degree. This is found to be cheaper than pay-

---

* In this instance not rites but lefts, an act of Ideological Significance applauded especially by Professors of History and Political Science, while Trustees squirm uncomfortably. Though leftist-leaning, the Professors try to stand up straight in the Academic Procession.

† Who begins by saying the Speaker needs no introduction and proceeds to such length that the introduction needs no Speaker.

‡ In many instances it is the audience that has come to the wrong conclusion.

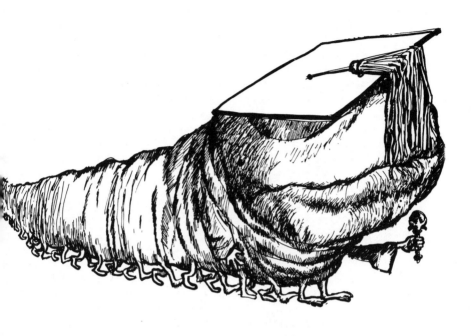

ing an Honorarium.* Actually such a degree is not given but conferred, with all the rights and privileges pertaining thereto, such as the recipient's being entitled to frame the degree and to hang the hood in a closet, thereby providing additional foodstuff for hungry moths.

After the Students in the Graduating Class have received their Earned Degrees, making them eligible to receive the Alumni *Newsletter,* there is a Benediction in which the Chaplain says a few well-chosen words about the Graduates, such as "God help them."

In a few more minutes, it now being late in the day, the Commencement goes into hiding for another year, knowing it will not be missed in the interval.

---

* An Honorarium is a large word for a small sum, while a Fee is a small word for a large sum.

The Curriculum

(Textus receptus) *

THE Curriculum is a large creature but little understood. It is so long that it stretches almost from one end of the Catalog to the other, leaving room only for the Calendar, the Faculty and Administration, and the Index, which are squeezed in before and after the lengthy and complicated Curriculum.

The size of the Curriculum is accounted for by its being full of Fields,† Disciplines, Departments, Requirements, Concentrations, and Prerequisites. At the heart of the Curriculum are the Courses, which are themselves full of esoteric little symbols, meaningful only to Academians, such

---

* The text approved by authorities in the area concerned. Actually the authorities are more concerned than the area.

† Almost all the Fields, in fact, except Elysian.

as 112a,b, MWF, and TTh. There may also be such cryptic words and expressions as "arranged," "half-course," and "May be repeated for credit." *

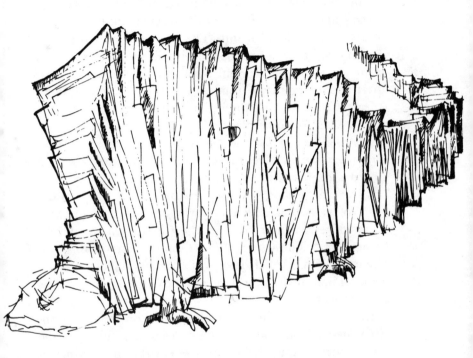

* To assume from "May be repeated for credit" that the average Student's credit is worth taking a chance on again would be risky, as the local bank manager knows.

The birth or creation of the Curriculum is somewhat unusual. A Dean or a Professor may say, "It was hammered out by the Educational Policy Committee." That would explain the strange sounds emanating from the Administration Building, as well as the bruised and dented look of the Curriculum, along with the patches and the obvious efforts to smooth it all out. There is no doubt the Curriculum has taken a beating, and it will probably take one again, since the Curriculum is given little rest but is torn apart and reorganized from time to time. It seems there is fear of its becoming too rigid. Also Change is in the air and looking for some place to light.

Another reason for the Curriculum's length is that it often becomes involved in a tug-of-war between the Old Guard and Forward-Looking members of the Faculty. Also involved in reshaping and restructuring the Curriculum are Professors that wish the Curriculum to be more job-oriented versus those wishing the Curriculum to have a broad base.* The Curriculum is sometimes said to be in a State of Flux, which is one of the larger states of Academe. Then again it is Under Study, something that is seldom over.

Every few years the Curriculum takes on an almost entirely new form, and every few years it returns to the form it had before it took on the entirely new form. In short, the more the Curriculum changes the more it remains the responsibility of Academians to change it until it is the same as it was.

One of the greatest satisfactions of a Senior Professor, as the new Curriculum begins to resemble the old, is muttering, *"Nunc pro tunc,"* meaning "Now for then," which, said over and over, sounds like a broken wagon wheel going around and around.

---

* A Professor with a broad base needs to cut down on sweets and starches and get more exercise.

The Custodian

(Sic eunt fata hominum) *

IN early times the Custodian was known as the Janitor.†
The Custodian is often stooped but rarely stupid. It is
stooped from looking for dirt and disorder in Academe.
It is almost never looking for trouble. In this respect it
differs from many Academians.

The Custodian shuffles slightly, especially when it is
close to retirement. Though it may not take early retirement, it retires early because it has to be at work before
any of the other creatures of Academe except the Grounds
Force.

---

* Such is the fate of man. As a matter of fact the Custodian is less
likely to have ulcers and diverticulitis than the President. In some ways
it has the best job in Academe. The only degrees it cares about are those
on the thermostat.

† Did you know that the word "Janitor" is related to Janus, the Latin
god of doors? The two kinds of doors (see the two faces of Janus) are of
course Indoors and Outdoors.

The Custodian carries a huge key ring with dozens of keys on it. You can hear it coming by the rattle and jangle of the keys. Only the Custodian has the key to every building and the intelligence to know which key fits which lock. If the Custodian fails to arrive, nothing can be done except to send out a search party, or if it is made up of Professors a research party, to look for the Custodian.

The Custodian keeps everything clean, except the Student Newspaper and some of the lectures in Sociology. The dirtiest thing on the Campus is the Underground Newspaper. In order to keep things clean, the Custodian has what looks like a bushy tail except that it has a handle on it and is pushed along in front instead of being dragged behind.

You can tell the Custodian from the Trustee by looking at its hands and especially at its fingernails, which give evidence of Honest Labor. It is the one creature that can not only work its way up but work its way down, from the top floor to the basement. It is usually in the basement that the Custodian can be found, if it can be found at all.

The Dean

(Deus ex machina) *

THE Dean is of a peculiar genus and can be found in several closely related genera. These are the Dean of Men, the Dean of Women, and the Dean of Faculty. They are alike in that they are all Deans, but except for a common † foxlike quality, they have noteworthy differences.

The Dean of Men, for instance, is itself male, while the Dean of Women is invariably female. It is hard to imagine a female Dean of Men or a male Dean of Women, though this is probably only a matter of time, the way things are changing in Academe. ‡

* God from the machine. As in drama (likewise removed from Reality), the Dean is made by the Machine (the Administration) to untangle plots and resolve crises.

† Though not necessarily vulgar.

‡ In Academe, Change is referred to as Progress by those who are responsible for making the Change.

The Dean of Men and the Dean of Women deal with Students, and sometimes deal harshly with them. When either of these Deans bares its teeth, at the same time bristling slightly, any Student that has been called before the Dean will be cowed.* As far as is known, no Student has ever been called *after* the Dean.

The Dean of Faculty keeps a list of Students, known as the Dean's List, but is more concerned with, as well as about, the Professors and the Curriculum. It has so much on its mind that its mind sags a little under the weight. The Dean of Faculty is a good example not of Mind over Matter but of Matter over Mind. It is constantly aware of the fact that it is next to the President, though the President may not be anywhere near. In fact when the President is at a great distance, perhaps at an Important Meeting, the Dean of Faculty may be Acting President, doing its best to play the role without makeup. Ultimately it may even become a President, a transformation that is highly possible in the Land of Academe. For there anything is possible, including the implausible and the unthinkable.

Mention has been made of the foxlike quality of all of the Deans. This is because of a Dean's sharp nose, which (at least so it says) it keeps to the grindstone. It uses its nose not only to track down Infractions of Rules or failure to keep Office Hours but to prick bubbles.†

Anything that gets by the Dean is foolproof. The fact that it has got by the Dean is proof enough.

---

* Watching a Student being cowed, gradually taking on bovine characteristics, is an interesting experience.

† These are made by Idealistic Students and by Professors who submit Unsolicited Proposals.

The Department Head

(Caput) *

DESPITE its name, the Department Head is more than merely a head. It also has a body of sorts, the sort varying considerably. However, it is its head or headship (it likes to be referred to as "Your Headship") that is most important.

It is not necessarily larger than the creatures under it but it seems so to those who are underneath and find that the Department Head blocks their view as well as their movement upward.†

The Department Head is sometimes called the Chairman or even the Rotating Chairman. It prefers to be

---

* *Caput,* the Latin word for head, should not be confused with the German *kaputt.* If languages could be mixed, however, we could have *kaputt caput,* or broken head, an expression which might come in handy.

† "Block Head!" they may mutter.

known as the Head, however, and not to have to rotate unless it wishes to. If it rotates it does so in a swivel chair that goes around and around but never gets anywhere. If a Professor sneaks in and is caught occupying the chair, the Department Head may throw the book at it, and the book will be a hardcover edition.

A peculiarity of the Department Head is the way the expression on its face changes. When the Department Head is talking to an Instructor or an Assistant Professor, its expression is one of condescension or scorn. But when it is talking to the Dean of the Faculty or the President, its expression is one of respect, mingled with envy. This expression is written all over its face, sometimes longhand but more often typed in triplicate.*

The Department Head's rivals are other Department Heads. Each Head has its own field and thinks the class on the other side of the fence is greener, i.e., less experienced, less knowledgeable, and less likely to be useful in Later Life. The Department Head will defend its own field to the death and is continually frightening off such sly encroachers as the Interdepartmental and the Interdisciplinary, which are always trying to inter.

---

* By its Secretary, which will do anything (almost) the Department Head desires.

The Dissertation

(Magno iam conatu magnas nugas) *

THE Dissertation usually comes after the Thesis. It does not come after the Thesis as a mad dog or a mugger might, but follows behind it at a discreet distance.† The Dissertation is a haughty, puffed-up creature. In its effort to look even larger than it is, and to overshadow the Thesis, it spreads itself out much as does the male peacock, extending, erecting, and spreading its tail feathers. ‡ The Dissertation goes to great lengths, the greater the better, and in spreading itself out often spreads itself thin.

* To produce tremendous trifles with great effort. The Dissertation, however, is not to be trifled with except by the Examining Committee.

† Timewise (a word to raise the Pedant's hackles), it often comes two or three years after the Thesis.

‡ Actually, as the Zoologist would be quick to tell you, these are not tail feathers but upper tail coverts.

51

With the help of its owner, the Candidate for a Ph.D., the Dissertation tries its best to look Learned. One way it does this is by gathering up scores of tiny creatures such as Ibids, Op Cits, Loc Cits, Supras, Infras, Et Seqs, Passims, Per Contras, and Nota Benes.* These swarm over and into the Dissertation like bees or ants, and the Reader is likely to be impressed and may even get stung.

The Dissertation is usually bound, but not bound and gagged. Eventually, or so the Candidate hopes, it will be approved. If it is not approved, the Candidate has three alternatives: (1) Revision, (2) Starting All Over, or (3) Taking Leave (perhaps of its senses).† If it is approved, though, the Dissertation will be filed away in the Library. "File away!" the order is given, and by the time the members of the Library Staff have finished with it, the poor Dissertation will have disappeared completely.

* And an occasional Sic, to show that all is not well.
† There is one other alternative, but it is beneath notice, which is why it is put at the bottom of the page. That is for the Candidate to settle for an A.B.D. (All But Dissertation), which is better than nothing but not much better.

The Donor

(De mortuis nil nisi bonum) *

THE Donor usually lives in the Outside World but is always welcome in Academe unless a Student Riot is in progress or a building named after the Donor is temporarily defaced by obscene graffiti.† In fact the Donor frequently receives an invitation to come to the Campus to hear a Conservative Speaker. Before the speech, the Donor is wined and dined (or perhaps only dined), being seated within earshot, or mouthshot, of the President and the Development. During the dinner the Donor is asked such searching questions as "What do you think of the weather we are having?" and "Did you bring your checkbook?"

---

* Say nothing but good about the dead. It is even more important to say nothing but good about the Donor while the Donor is still alive and earning.

† Or Modern Art. Sometimes it is hard to tell which is which.

The Donor is somewhat like a plant, in that it is constantly being cultivated. There is, however, no special season for cultivation. This goes on the year around, interrupted only by times of harvest, when the President and the Development may be seen rubbing the palms of their hands in anxious anticipation and occasionally referring to a large chart on the wall entitled "Current Budget." They are counting (as high as possible) on the Donor to erase the Deficit, an ugly red line that lurks menacingly in the lower right-hand corner.

Of the various species of Donor, the most popular with the President and the Development is one that has some connection with the College or University, being an Old Grad or the parent, or better still the ailing grandparent, of a present Student. This causes its heartstrings to hang out, along with its purse strings, and they can be easily grasped and tugged until something (preferably the Donor) gives.

Of all the Old Grads, the one making the most attractive Donor is the Very Old Grad, with a short life expectancy. The secret vice of the Development is to haunt the obituary columns, especially when it knows of a Donor whose will, when last it heard, was wavering.

Each night the Development prays that the stock market will be up and the Donor in good spirits though not necessarily in good health. *"La donna è mobile,"* as the Italians say, meaning that the Donor, especially the female Donor, is fickle and easily moved from one Good Cause to another. What is important is getting to the Donor first and getting from the Donor the most.*

---

* The more the better if Professors are going to remain satisfied, i.e., to be paid more and more for teaching less and less.

The Dorm

(Virtus dormitiva) *

THE Dorm is of no one shape,† but of many shapes. Sometimes it is square, sometimes it is round, sometimes it is
squatty, sometimes it towers high. Sometimes it has wings,
but no one has ever seen a Dorm fly. ‡

The two main types of Dorm are the Co-Ed Dorm and
the Single-Sex Dorm. The Single-Sex Dorm is either all
male or all female, except during Open Hours, which in
earlier times lasted only briefly, perhaps Sunday afternoon,

* Power to induce sleep. Though the Dorm is intended as a place for
sleeping, it provides so many other activities for Students that the Classroom has largely taken over this function.

† Though it may be in bad shape.

‡ What you may be thinking of is a House Fly, but a House is not a
Home and a Dorm is not a House, or it is not supposed to be, though it
may have a Housemother or Housekeeper.

instead of all night, and was known as Open House. Open House was carefully supervised by a species that was long endangered and is now extinct in Academe, the Chaperone. During Open Hours there is no telling what goes on, or rather there is no one telling what goes on. This is not prudery but prudence.

The Dorm is teeming, or infested, with Occupants. These run all over and in and out, but the Dorm is at their mercy and unable to do anything about them. No matter what the Occupants do, the Dorm is dormant. Sometimes, however, an Occupant or an Outsider will go too far, setting fire to a portion of the Dorm and perhaps even gutting it (burning its guts). The reason for such an act is often unknown, since such an act is unreasonable. The worst part about it (assuming it is covered not only by wood and plaster but by insurance) is that it causes Undesirable Publicity. Book burning by some is thought de-

sirable, but these are the very ones who are most outraged by Dorm burning.*

However, most Occupants do nothing more to the Dorm than stick thumbtacks into it and decorate it with unmentionable graffiti which is hardly worth mentioning. Usually a Dorm has a longer life than most of its Occupants and might live indefinitely if it were not Condemned. Once it has been Condemned, the Dorm goes down very rapidly and soon disappears. Its Occupants, which have been living off their parents, may now be forced to live Off Campus.†

---

* Having a burning desire is something else. Oddly, the desire itself is not burned.

† This helps put an end to the madness of parents, known as *in loco parentis,* who have been marching around carrying a banner on two sticks, or a Double Standard.

The Economist

(Radix malorum est cupiditas) *

AMONG the creatures of Academe, the Economist is probably best at juggling. Even while keeping its eyes fixed on the Charts, Graphs, and Statistical Tables with which it is surrounded, it juggles Figures.† It does this partly to display its skill and partly to justify its Predictions, especially when there is a small error, up to 90 percent, in what it predicted.

The Economist usually has a concerned look, being concerned about business concerns. Privately, it is also con-

---

* It would be nice if this could be translated "The root of evil is stupidity," but then it would apply to Academians generally and not just to the Economist.

† It is curious that, while there are Statistical Tables, there are no Statistical Chairs. That is why the Economist remains standing, or tries to retain its standing, though it sometimes counsels "sitting it out."

cerned about Private Enterprise, which must always be on guard against that insidious creature, Creeping Inflation. The Economist must also cope with such giant beasts as Big Business, the Corporation, the Conglomerate, and, the largest and grossest of all, the GNP, or Gross National Product.*

Often the Economist is found on a sort of teeter-totter, known as the Balance of Trade, which is not only up and down but favorable and unfavorable. Another exhilarating experience is riding the Dow Jones during a rising and falling Market. Much as the Economist is interested in Production, often having a large family, it is also interested in Consumption.† Unless producers produce, consumers will have nothing to consume; and unless consumers consume, producers will have no reason to produce. It is as simple as that, although the Economist has ways of making it seem more complicated.

The Economist may or may not know that the word "pecuniary" comes from the Latin *pecus,* meaning cattle. The Romans bought things with cows instead of money, but ran into difficulty when someone wanted to buy an inexpensive item, such as a secondhand chariot wheel or a Christian, and the seller couldn't make the change. So it was that money came into being, and money led to such things as Foreign Exchange, Devaluation, Inflation, and courses in "Monetary Theory" and "Money and Banking." ‡

* No, the largest is the National Debt, but that is too large for the Academian, or anyone else, to grasp.

† The Economist makes a distinction between Consumption and Tuberculosis.

‡ In the old days, when cows were used for currency, they were kept not in banks but in barns. An advantage of present-day money is that it doesn't have to be fed. (The Fed is something for the Government to explain.) It is true that we still refer to small amounts of money as chicken feed.

The Economist teaches Students about Business Cycles, which are riskier even than Motor Cycles, and such concepts as Free Enterprise and Planned Economy. Planned Parenthood is left to the Sociologists and Plant Parenthood to the Botanists.

Since it is so much interested in money, it is no wonder that the Economist in addition to being a Professor is usually a Consultant. This is what is known in Academe as Moonlighting. Not wishing to be seen by less fortunate colleagues in English and Philosophy, creatures in which Government and Industry have no interest, the Economist disguises itself in a gray flannel suit and sallies forth after dark. It may not be at its best the next morning when teaching a first-period class in Introduction to Economics, but that bulge in the inside pocket of its tweed jacket, the jacket with the scholarly leather patches on the elbows, is a reassuring wad of currency. It is known as a Consultant's Fee, and is one of the benefits of the fee-enterprise system.

The Emeritus

(Stat magni nominis umbra) *

THEY say of the Emeritus that it has been put out to pasture, having been horsing around long enough. This would seem an inviting prospect, with nothing to do but ruminate, but the Emeritus has time on its hands.† Unlike horses that are retired in the Outside World, the Emeritus is not made use of on something comparable to a stud farm. It has its dreams, of course, such as the one of the curvaceous Student that came into its office and offered to do anything for an A. Or, once it got Tenure, of telling the Dean where it could go.

---

* He stands, the mere shadow of a great name. At least this is better than being shadowed by certain members of the Department that were looking for an excuse to force their colleague into Early Retirement and improve their chances for promotion.

† Or, rather, on its wrist: the watch it was given at its Retirement Party.

But it also has its nightmares, as of the article it published in a Learned Journal that was discovered to have been based on a Student's term paper. Or of making a motion in a Faculty Meeting that was considered obscene. When it faces Reality, however, it realizes that it is going downhill, which is an uphill battle. It also makes the appalling discovery that it is getting older every year. However instead of saying, "I am getting older" it says,

"I am not getting any younger," which is just as true and has a more optimistic sound to it.

At any rate, the Emeritus now has time to think, something it has not done for years, and it thinks of things it should have thought of before. It is aware of Descartes' famous statement, *"Cogito, ergo sum,"* which is usually translated as "I think, therefore I am." But something has been lost in translation, which is a second *"cogito."* What Descartes really had in mind was "I think, therefore I am, I think." Or, in the complete text, it could mean, "I think, therefore I am Cogito," which would seem a better name for a thinker or cogitator than Descartes.

The Emeritus can at last get back to work on its Project, which it had been keeping in Abeyance, a large receptacle from which many things never emerge. It takes out its Project every day and dusts it off and fondles it fondly and then puts it back. Without its Project, it says, it would be lost, and yet if the Project were lost it would feel a certain sense of relief, since it would have a good reason for not doing anything, which is what it had actually been looking forward to doing.*

The one thing that troubles the Emeritus, apart from Advancing Years,† is being replaced by an Academian that, despite its youth and lack of experience, is doing the job quite as well as the Emeritus did. If the truth be told, the callow, inexperienced replacement is doing it better. Fortunately the truth is seldom told, or not within hearing of the Emeritus.

---

* Whether not doing anything is the same as doing nothing is a Moot Point. Most points in Academe are moot, which means that, like Academic Questions, they are pointless.

† Have you ever heard of Retreating Years?

The Exam

(Prospectus horrendus) *

THE Exam is related to the Test † and the Quiz, but is larger and fiercer than either of these. It lies in wait for the Student and waits for the Student to lie. So determined is the Exam that it keeps the Student not only from prevaricating but from vacillating and equivocating. The Student may try to get around the Exam by some such means as Circumlocution, but rarely succeeds. Then again it may seek Postponement, pleading illness or even death. ‡

---

* Horrible prospect. Yet, as Students know, it must be faced. This is doubly difficult for the two-faced Student that has spent more time trying to make a Good Impression than studying.

† Interestingly, the Latin *testis*, meaning a witness or one who attests, in the plural is *testes*.

‡ This requires the Student to present a signed statement by a physician or mortician.

Some would describe the Exam as being like a ferocious police dog, athwart the onward and upward path of the Student and, being athwart, thwarting its progress. (It seems to have a slight lithp.) However, the Student has been heard to say, "I have taken the Exam." From the grim look of the Student as it says this, it would appear that taking an Exam is like taking strong, bitter medicine. Subsequently the Student may say, happily, "I passed the Exam." This further substantiates the medical parallel, since passing the Exam apparently removes an obstruction and gives relief comparable to that felt in passing a kidney stone.

Sometimes, though, the Student says, with a long face, "I failed the Exam." * The Exam will then be described as too tough, too long, too specific, too vague, or too dreadful for words. Putting too and too together, a fellow Student may make some such consoling remark as "Too bad."

There are several species of the Exam. One is the True-False, which according to the Law of Averages gives the Student a 50-percent chance of passing even if the Student is totally, instead of only partially, ignorant. Another is the Multiple Choice, which is a little like Multiple Sclerosis and can be fatal. Still another is the Essay, which provides the Student with more opportunity for evasive action but is wasteful of ink and paper. This type of Exam is the most difficult for the Professor, since it calls for Subjective Judgments. These take longer than making check marks and may cause the Professor to put in an honest day's work.†

The Exam is probably the most hated creature in

---

* Or it may say, tersely, "I flunked." If several Exams have been flunked, the Student may flunk out. There is no known case of a Student having flunked in.

† A dishonest day's work is something to think about.

Academe. It has been seen how it stands in the way of the Student and how it exacts work, no matter how inexact, from the Professor. No wonder the Exam, like the Grade and the Requirement, is less and less encountered and may disappear from Academe altogether. If this happens, it will become only a Memory, being replaced by that paper tiger, the Paper. The Paper, while long and imposing, can come straight from a book, if the book is not widely known,* or from a helpful agency that advertises in the campus newspaper. The Student that has learned how to produce a Paper without writing it is ready to take on the Thesis and even the Dissertation.

So the Paper leads to bigger and better things, or at least bigger things, while the Exam is a Dead End.

* I.e., by the Professor.

The Frat

(Quae fuerunt vitia mores sunt) *

THE Frat looks somewhat like the Dorm, though smaller. Some consider it a Club, but not the kind that is used by the Campus Security Force to discourage the Riot, the Rip-off, and the Rape.† The female counterpart or sister of the Frat is the Soror, or Sorority. The Soror does many of the same things as the Frat, or as many as it can, considering its facilities.

The Frat is a relaxed, kindly creature that thrives on intercourse. ‡ Male Students seek it out and are happy to get into it. In fact they become the Frat's members, thus

---

* What once were thought vices are now the usual thing. The Old Grad is both shocked and envious.

† Which have replaced, in Academe, the earlier three R's.

‡ Social intercourse, of course.

providing it with arms and legs it would otherwise lack. It is difficult to determine whether the Students belong to the Frat or the Frat belongs to the Students.

At any rate, such Students wear a Frat pin, which is like a safety pin, not in appearance but in the safety or self-assurance it affords those able to afford it. It is a sign of Having Arrived, even though it is also worn when away from the Frat, after having departed.

Because of its opening and closing its mouth to let Students in and out, the Frat resembles a fish feeding on worms, flies, and other creatures it finds tasty. The likeness is heightened by its top or back, its shingles resembling scales. Just what the Students do inside the Frat is not known. They are obviously not digested, since they emerge intact from the same end as the one by which they entered.

It is considered Prestigious to have been taken into a Frat by those who have not been taken in. However, many of those who have not been taken in think that those who were taken in were taken in, though they may be mistaken in taking this view.

There are usually two or three Greek letters on the face of the Frat. For most Students today this is the extent of their knowledge of Greek.

The Full Professor

(Ad ultimum) *

THE most impressive of all the kinds of Professors is the Full Professor. It is not apparent at first glance precisely what it is full of, but there is an obvious fullness. In fact it is so full that it seems ready to burst. It may, however, only be bursting with pride. At a closer look or, better, upon dissection, it will be seen that the Full Professor is full of such things as Information, Experience, and Authority. There may also be bites and pieces of Instructors, Assistant Professors, and Associate Professors it has chewed out or devoured because of its insatiable appetite to rise to the Top Rank and they got in the way.

The Full Professor is also full of satisfaction. Unless it goes into Administration, it is everything a Professor can

* At last, finally. Or, as it may say of itself, "They should have given it to me years ago."

hope to be. Of course it is also a Scholar, as may be seen by the brown patches on its elbows.* In fact it is probably a Productive Scholar. Every time it produces anything it gives a copy of it to those in its Field and to the President. In order to do this, it is forced to reproduce what it produces. In the Field of Scholarship, reproduction is done with a machine and has nothing to do with sex, although the Full Professor has a Large Bibliography.

The Full Professor sits on numerous Committees. As if this were not enough, it often chairs a Committee. The Committee that has been sat on and chaired as often as once a month is, understandably, in bad shape and unable to do much.

When it is not sitting on a Committee, the Full Professor is usually to be found in its orifice, which is its nesting place except that it is not supposed to sleep there and does so only briefly and while pretending to be actively doing something, such as thinking. It may occupy a Name Chair, which has on it the name of the Donor. One would think it would have its own name on it, but that is not the way things are done in Academe. A Name Chair is Impressive and, more important, it pays better. Only in Academe does a Chair pay, and then only when it is occupied.

It is no wonder that in time the Full Professor becomes Emeritus.†

---

* Proof of the fact that it spends much time in a brown study. Or perhaps it has elbowed its way through a crowd of competitors.

† And goes from a Name Chair to a rocking chair, though some think that by now it is off its rocker.

The Grind

(Nil sine magno vita labore dedit mortalibus) *

THE Grind is a species, or in view of its lowly status a subspecies, of the Student. Because of its slow movement it resembles a turtle or tortoise,† although the slowness is more apparent in its brain than in its appendages. It continues to press forward, confident that it will ultimately arrive, even though it may be uncertain of where it is going or why.

Almost everything about the Grind is somewhat low. ‡ It has a low I.Q., a low Percentile, a low Achievement, a

---

* Life has given nothing to mortals without much labor. This has no application, of course, to the very bright and the very lucky, neither of which the Grind is.

† The distinction between a turtle and a tortoise is a matter of Great Importance to an Academian.

‡ It may, though, have high Aspirations.

low Verbal, a low Math, and a low profile. Other Students, however, also have something low: a low opinion of the Grind. The Grind has no expectation of passing them, much less surpassing them, but hopes to pass a Course now and then.

The Grind can seldom be heard laughing. This is either because the Grind has no sense of humor or because it has no time for anything frivolous. It needs every minute if it is to complete an Assignment or cover a Course.* If it sometimes fails to get the point of a Professor's remark, it may not be the fault of the Grind. The remark may be pointless.

The Grind takes Copious Notes, hoping to absorb them later but having no opportunity because of the need to take more Copious Notes. By the time it has covered a Course it is itself covered by Notes, a performance it considers noteworthy but often finds to be of No Avail. This is when the Low Grades come out, having been lurking in the Registrar's office awaiting the time to pounce. The Grind is terrified of Low Grades, and the Low Grades know it. *"Gradus ad Parnassum!"* or "Grades, go back to Parnassus!" the Grind may scream, beside itself † with fear.‡

The Grind is known as Atypical, which does not mean A Typical Student but the opposite. This is confusing to anyone not familiar with the language of Academe, where the opposite of "opposite" is "apposite." §

* In Academe, a Course is always covered. If it were uncovered, something might be discovered.

† That makes two Grinds.

‡ "Back to the Grind," other Students say. What they have in mind is not joining the Grind but watching a stripteaser at a nightclub.

§ This interesting fact was copied verbatim, *ceteris paribus,* from the Grind's Copious Notes.

The Historian

(Ante hoc, ergo propter hoc) *

A curious thing about the Historian is that its head is on backward. Therefore as the Historian goes forward it is always looking back. Usually, however, it stays where it is or goes forward very slowly, being too busy looking back to do anything else.

Sometimes the Historian turns around so that its head is facing the way it is going, thus walking backward while going forward. But this it finds awkward and uncomfortable.† It prefers the Past to the Present and the Future. Occasionally the Historian will try to convince its colleagues in Academe that the best way to know where you

---

* Before this, therefore in consequence of this. The change of *post* to *ante* introduces an interesting idea. If anyone can understand it, which I doubt, the Historian can.

† Yet it may aid its research, causing it to stumble on something.

are going is to keep looking at where you have been. It may even assert that it knows more about the Future than they do because it knows more about the Past.

The Historian has unusual eyes. They stick out of its head like telescopes. As a result, the Historian has a good view of the Distant Past but is unable to see what is directly under its eyes, such as Yesterday and Last Week. The Historian usually fastens its telescopic eyes on some particular object in the Past, such as the Medieval Period. A period, which to the Grammarian is a small dot, to the Historian is a large and important area.

It is a large area, that is, until Specialization sets in. This is a condition a little like Astigmatism or Tunnel Vision, which causes the Historian to see a smaller and smaller part of the Period. Curiously, the farther the Historian gets from the Past the more clearly it sees it. But, since it has more and more difficulty seeing the Immediate Past, there are those who wish its telescopic eyes were fitted with bifocals.

Such Academians, with their faces facing forward, think the Historian is looking the wrong way. Some of them, known as the Cynics, even mutter, "What you learn from Historians is that you don't learn from Historians." *

---

* Now that there are more female Historians, there should probably be an appropriate word for them, such as Herstorians. A History buff, by the way, is a lover of History and not an Historian who shows off by going around in the buff.

The Instructor

(In limine) *

THE Instructor will be found on the bottom rung of the
Academic Ladder, looking up wistfully and starry-eyed at
the Assistant Professor, Associate Professor, and Full Professor. The only creature lower is the Teaching Assistant,
which has not yet placed a foot, or a hand, on the precious
Ladder. Though the Instructor is in a low position, it has
high hopes. Each night it dreams of ascending the Ladder,
step by step, until it reaches Academic Heaven † as a Full
Professor with Tenure. Each morning comes the rude
awakening to the fact that it is only an Instructor, without Tenure, Sabbatical, or Publications.

* On the threshold. Actually the Instructor is over the threshold and
inside the Teaching Profession, but just barely.

† Where there are few harps but many who harp, as well as carp and
cavil. What they harp on, without a harp to harp on, is too complicated
to go into here.

What keeps the Instructor going, though not necessarily upward, is interest in Students and love of teaching. The Instructor came to Academe with the idealistic belief that a Dedicated Teacher would be admired, respected, and given Quick Advancement. It soon learned, alas, that to most Deans and Professors, as well as members of the APT Committee, teaching though desirable is a Minor Consideration.* In the Outside World there is the saying, "Those who can, do; those who can't, teach." In Academe

---

* There is nothing especially apt about the APT, or Committee on Appointment, Promotion, and Tenure. The Committee is an unusual kind of jury, consisting entirely of judges who pass judgment on Academians who, oddly, are in Academe but have not yet Arrived.

this is slightly altered to "Those who can, publish; those who can't, teach." It is sometimes further altered to "Those who can, publish; those who can't teach, teach." *

When the Instructor arrives in Academe it is given a small hole or burrow, known as an Office. It is not expected to live there but only to stay there during its Office Hours. There is a pane of glass in the door so that the Department Head can look in and be sure the Instructor is there when it is supposed to be there.† It also enables the Department Head to see whether the Instructor, if a male, is with a female Student and, if so, what progress they are making.

The Instructor is always eager to leave its Office and go to class. For one thing, it grows weary of reading the graffiti written on the walls by previous occupants, such as "Publish or parish—I went into the ministry" and "Profs shouldn't make passes at girls in their classes."

But mainly it wishes to go to class because there it can watch Young Minds unfold. It can lecture and know it is being listened to, unless the notes being written are intended for another Student, carrying some such message as "How about tonight?" It can also ask questions and be asked questions. In the latter case, if it does not know the answer it can answer the question with another question, most often "What do *you* think?" This gives the Instructor time to gather its wits, which are all over the place.

The greatest challenge to an Instructor is not to tell everything it knows about a subject in fifty minutes. A little something must be left over for the rest of the Semester.

---

* Or, in Education, teach teachers to teach.

† There is no pane of glass in the office door of a Distinguished Professor, since it may be assumed that such a Professor is away or, if there, could not be distinguished.

The Librarian

(Librarius, liberalis, libertas, et cetera) *

THE Librarian is related to the Bookworm.† In fact it was probably a Bookworm as a Student and unquestionably a worm of some sort in Library School. But it emerged from its vermicular state and appeared as a winged creature, resembling a butterfly or moth. Fluttering about from book to book and from reader to reader, the Librarian is careful not to move its wings too rapidly or to bat them (there are those who think some Librarians *are* Bats) against anything, lest it make a Noise.

---

* Library, liberal, liberty, and so forth. All of these words go back to the Latin *liber*, but there is a pronounced difference. The difference between *liber*, book and *liber*, free is that one has a short "i" and one has a long "i." That may be why books are free at a library but a librarian is not always free to purchase or circulate certain books.

† But not, as one might think, to the Bookkeeper, a species actually hated by the Librarian.

A Noise * is what it abhors most, especially in that sacred area of the Library known as the Reading Room. There the loudest sound heard is the Librarian's "Shh!" a sibilant stricture that resembles a sudden gust of wind or a wave subsiding sensuously on the sandy seashore. The comparison with a wave is probably more apt, since the Librarian's "Shh!" usually drowns out the whispers, chair scrapings, coughs, and gum-poppings of Readers.

The Librarian, whether male or female, is almost always in love. It is not in love with other Librarians, though it likes them well enough, but with Books. Often, becoming a Bibliophile, it projects its dainty feelers and voluptuously feels a Volume from its jacket to its flyleaf and from its frontispiece to its End. It may even reach in and touch its Appendix. The satisfaction it gets is beyond description and therefore will not be described here.

What disturbs the Librarian almost as much as a Noise is finding a book that has been mistreated or, even worse, misplaced—wrongly shelved by some do-it-yourshelf reader. Of course the Librarian itself may deflower a book, removing a flower that has been pressed or used as a bookmark. Such a book may in addition be Overdue.

The Librarian silently flits about from the Card Catalog, which is used to catalog cards, to the Stacks. The latter are not really stacks, since books are not stacked but neatly placed on shelves side by side. If they were actually stacked in stacks in the Stacks, no creature in Academe would be so distressed as the Librarian.†

With reference to the Librarian, we should not overlook the Reference Librarian. This is a species of Librarian that flourishes on Tracking Things Down and is so good at Sources that it is thought to be a magician or Sourcerer.

---

* Also known, by the Librarian, as a Racket or a Disturbance.
† The Librarian, if a female, may itself be well stacked.

Finally there is the Rare Book Librarian that, devouring books, likes them rare. Oddly, most books that are rare are also well-done. *De gustibus non est disputandum,* or for this reason there is no accounting for the taste.*

* According to Francis Bacon, "Some books are to be tasted, others swallowed, and some few to be chewed and digested." As the Librarian knows, books that are swallowed but neither chewed nor digested can cause trouble, especially those that are bound in leather or buckram.

The Linguist

(Copia verborum) *

THE Linguist speaks with a foreign tongue. It may even have at its command several foreign tongues, and at its command they do its bidding.† These foreign tongues, which fill its mouth to overflowing, it did not import but picked up while abroad on a Fulbright, Guggenheim, or Volkswagen.

Though the Linguist commands several foreign tongues, there is one which is its Specialty. This is the tongue it teaches, though it would seem that the tongue already knows all it needs to know. The Linguist uses this tongue at every opportunity. ‡ It also gives Private Lessons, mak-

---

* Torrent of words, fluency. It isn't what the Academian says that is important, it is the number of languages it can say it in.

† The Linguist may be at a book auction, bidding for some such exciting work as *Grammaire de l'Ancien Français* or *Anekdoten von Friedrich dem Grossen.*

‡ Unfortunately, opportunities are limited, even in Academe.

ing sure that no one is around to see or hear what is going on.

The Linguist divides its Specialty, the tongue in which it is Fluent, into three parts: Elementary, Intermediate, and Advanced. The Advanced is the part that sticks out the farthest. Even Students that get to the Advanced do not satisfy the Linguist, which is forever calling attention to their Pronunciation and their Small Vocabulary. The Linguist has a Large Vocabulary. On the other hand, or wherever, it has no Accent. This is a condition greatly admired, especially by the Linguist, which loves to be called upon to show its Facility.

If the Linguist is truly illustrious, it has not only several foreign tongues but Decorations from heads of state. These Decorations it wears inconspicuously in a conspicuous place on its chest. If you ask the Linguist to explain the significance of each Decoration, it will tell you at length, as well as breadth.*

The Linguist is proud of its ability to roll its *r*'s, but may say scornfully of others, less proficient, that they do not know their *r*'s from a hole in the ground.

* Despite its many tongues, the Linguist never becomes either tongue-tied or tongue-tired.

The Lit Prof

(Literatim, verbatim, punctuatim) *

THE Lit Prof is also known as a Man of Letters, but unlike the Postman it delivers not letters but Papers. These it delivers to the Modern Language Association and similar groups. Membership in such organizations is based on one important qualification: ability to pay the Annual Dues.

Usually the Lit Prof is seen holding a book. If it is holding the book in such a position that the title and name of the author are clearly visible, it is probably a book of which it is the author or coauthor. It may even be a book that has been "adopted" by some creature which, unlike the author, is unable to give birth to anything as hard to get out as a large tome with sharp corners.†

---

* Letter for letter, word for word, period for period. This is obviously incomplete, making no reference to the faulty reference or the dangling participle.

† "I am getting out a book," the Lit Prof says just before going into labor.

The Lit Prof begins by teaching Freshman English, and though a Ph.D. rather than an M.D. pays close attention to such personal matters as the use and abuse of the colon. Of all the creatures of Academe, it has the most bloodshot eyes. These are the result of reading Student Compositions, some of which are badly decomposed. The Lit Prof proffers both a Grade and a Comment. If it is hesitant about giving a D it may instead give a C-minus-minus, the two minuses indicating that it is a very low C indeed but far better than a D-plus. The Comment is intended to explain what the Student should have written instead of what it wrote, or in other words what the Lit Prof would have written had the Lit Prof been writing on the assignment assigned by the Lit Prof. The Comment would be more helpful if the Student were able to read the Lit Prof's handwriting.*

Later the Lit Prof teaches the Survey, and feels itself master of all it surveys. Of great help to it is the Syllabus, which tells it where it should be at any given time. For instance on October 26 it should be on Donne, if it is a Semester Course, and when it is done with Donne it should be on Milton. As it often says, "If it's Tuesday, it must be Keats." Each Student has its own Syllabus, which it carries about and uses instead of a calendar, mindful of Shakespeare's famous words, "To the last Syllabus of recorded time."

Eventually the Lit Prof, having published enough articles in the Learned Journals, where the yawn comes up like thunder, is an Authority and can teach what it knows, whether or not it is worth knowing. Indeed the Lit Prof is widely recognized for its perceptive work, *The Use of the Parenthetical Expression in the Novels of Henry James*, and its even more admired four-volume biography of

---

* A Marginal Comment, on the edge of being understandable.

Thomas Chatterton, provokingly entitled *A Long Study of a Short Life.** How it got from Henry James to Thomas Chatterton is the subject of another book which, as they say, has been "in the works" for eight years and may yet be completed if the Lit Prof can remember where it put the manuscript.†

The other Professors envy the Lit Prof. Though red-eyed and stooped, it gets paid for reading books that they read for pleasure. What they fail to realize is that when a book is read to be taught, the pleasure is dissipated and so, sometimes, is the Lit Prof. Those red eyes may not be from reading but from doing whatever it does to keep from reading.

The Lit Prof does not read as others do but constantly looks for Symbolism and Hidden Meanings. This it does by Reading Between the Lines, which requires discipline and concentration. Even Shakespeare's *Plays* become work, just as his *Works* are largely plays.

The reason the Lit Prof prefers to interpret the works of earlier writers, such as Spenser and Milton, is that these writers are long since dead and therefore unlikely to exclaim, after reading an article by the Lit Prof, "I meant no such thing!" Sometimes, however, the Lit Prof may dare to interpret the works of living writers, hoping they are too busy writing or proofreading or making lecture tours to read the Quarterly in which the interpretation appears.

---

* Both are University Press publications, subsidized by a Grant from the National Foundation for the Advancement of Professors.

† So far it has looked everywhere but on its desk, the task of digging through accumulated papers being too formidable.

The Mathematician

(Problemata, problemata) *

FORTUNATELY the Mathematician has ten fingers. This
makes it possible for it to count to ten without using an
abacus or a computer. It also has ten toes, which enables
it to count to a total of twenty, and it is well on its way.
Only in Higher Mathematics does the Mathematician need
to count the hairs on its head.

So far we have been concerned only with Arithmetic,
which includes addition, subtraction, multiplication, and
division. Most of this (even multiplication, unlike most
species) the Mathematician can do in its head, which saves
blackboards, chalk, erasers, and no telling what else. It is
when the Mathematician gets into Algebra, Geometry,
Trigonometry, and Calculus that things get complicated.

---

* Problems, problems. Without Problems to solve, the Mathematician
and its Students would have nothing to do.

In Algebra, for instance, it is important to discover what *x* equals, and what is remarkable is that so many care. The Mathematician knows, but all it will say is something cryptic, such as "$x^2-y^2 = (x-y) (x+y)$." *

More trouble is in store for the Student when the Mathematician tries to explain Geometry, in which there is a relationship, or so the Mathematician says, between lines, points, and planes. Students also get all tangled up with circles, squares, and triangles, the last being especially meaningful if two boys fall in love with the same girl.

* It has the answers in the back of the book, the cheat.

One solution is for her to give her hand, or whatever, to the first one to figure out the value of *pi*.*

When the Mathematician gets into Trigonometry and Calculus, most Students are lost, unless they are carrying a Slide Rule, which is as important to the Mathematician as a compass to a mariner or an Athletic Supporter to an Athlete. Among other things, a Slide Rule if slid properly and logarithmically will extract a square root or even a cube root, and is therefore useful in the garden.

As any Mathematician will tell you, not only Physics and Astronomy but such fields as Statistics and even Life Insurance could not get along without Mathematics. Indeed, thanks to Mathematics it is not only possible to calculate the probabilities of life expectancy but to aim an artillery piece so that the figures come out right, or at any rate stop moving.

Usually the Mathematician has little interest in Poetry. Therefore despite acknowledging a debt to Euclid and finding figures fascinating, it probably cannot quote Edna St. Vincent Millay's famous "Euclid alone has looked on Beauty bare." With such a distraction, it is amazing that Euclid could have kept his mind on theorems and written *Elements of Geometry,* used as a textbook for two thousand years. Students might have enjoyed it more, however, had it contained a centerfold photo of Beauty.†

If no mention has been made in the above regarding the Old Math and the New Math, it is because there are no Old Mathematicians and New Mathematicians—just Old and Young.

---

* Or to know that Archimedes originally worked this out, or that *pi* is the sixteenth letter of the Greek alphabet. But if you are not a Mathematician and are dying to know, the value of *pi* is approximately 3.14159265, a figure of less importance to the male Student than 38-23-36.

† Euclid is often called the Father of Geometry. No one seems to know who the mother was.

The Musician

(Virginibus puerisque canto) *

THOUGH several creatures of Academe, especially Administrators, might lay claim to being the nosiest, there can
be no doubt that the Musician is the noisiest. Unless, that
is, it is a Musicologist, a species that has such a reputation
for knowing about the history and science of Music that
it does not wish to spoil it all by playing "Chopsticks" on
the piano, no matter how well.†

Then of course there is the Composer, not always known
for its composure. It is often temperamental, flying into
a High Dudgeon when Inspiration will not come or when
its Composition is not appreciated. The Composer can be

---

* I sing for girls and boys. This was said by Horace in one of his *Odes*,
though most think of Horace (I forget his last name) not as a singer but
as a poet.

† By the way, have you ever heard "Chopsticks" played on a violin?

recognized by its foreign accent and by the fact that it wears its hair long even when long hair is out of fashion with Students. This makes it easier for it to tear its hair when it is in a creative frenzy. It is always writing notes. These, however, are musical notes and no reply is expected. Nonetheless the Composer may be said to have "left its stamp" on the Music of its generation.

The Musician generally plays an instrument and teaches Students how to play it. The instrument may be a piano, a violin, a trumpet, a bassoon, or even, for those optimistic about their Afterlife, a harp. During the Elementary Course, the Musician tries hard not to let the Student see its grimaces of pain, and may stuff cotton in its ears or, if near Retirement, keep its hearing aid turned off. As much as possible the Musician locks the Student in a soundproof room, known as a Practice Room,* where the only eardrums it can damage are its own.

Sometimes the Musician eschews instruments, which at least is better than chewing them, and teaches Voice. It should have a good Voice itself. If a male Musician, it has a bass, baritone, or tenor, and if a female Musician a contralto, soprano, or ear-piercing scream. The Musician teaches the Student how to breathe, if it has not already learned this fundamental principle, and how to hold a note without using its hands. In fact the Musician may press in on the Student's diaphragm, especially if it is a male Musician and the Student is a female that has a diaphragm that requires attention. Pressing any other protruding parts may elicit screams, moans, or other sounds which may not do much for the Student's Musical Education but may help its Education in general.

If one Voice is not enough, the Musician may gather up

* Practice in this instance not making Perfect.

a group of singers and form a Glee Club or a Choir. The difference between the two is largely that the Glee Club sings somewhat bawdier songs and, unlike the Choir, is not invited to sing in College Church. Anyhow, it does better with the Alma Mater than with the Hallelujah Chorus. An advantage of either the Glee Club or the Choir is that the good Voices can drown out the bad Voices.* Also the Musician, now called the Conductor, can show its courage, and sometimes a rip in its old tuxedo, by turning its back on the audience.

A parallel with the Glee Club and Choir is the Orchestra. Here also there is hoped-for strength in numbers, and instruments (not intentionally instruments of torture) are employed instead of Voices. Once again the Musician takes on the role of the Conductor. Mounting a podium, a small platform which makes it possible for it to overlook mistakes, and holding a baton (Latin *bastum,* a stick, related in a roundabout way to our word "bastard"), it threatens any member of the Orchestra if it gets off tempo. "I'll give you the beat!" it threatens menacingly.

The Musician is frowned upon by most Members of the Faculty because an F to it means *forte* and an FF *fortissimo.* But the Musician frowns back, knowing it can make a living in the Outside World if necessary—something the Philosopher and the Lit Prof would find difficult.

* Unfortunately, the opposite can also occur.

The Ph.D.

(Sine qua non)

THE name of the Ph. D. is deceptive. One would expect it to be pronounced "Fu-dee," but actually it is pronounced "Pee-aitch-dee," with the accent on the "Pee." This is perhaps because of fear (often legitimate) of being confused with a "fuddy" or a "fuddy-duddy."

The Ph.D. is conceived and delivered with considerable difficulty and pain. The period of gestation is usually several years. It is no wonder, therefore, that the possessor of a Ph.D., which it displays to all who come within sight or hearing, is inordinately proud. The Ph.D. means little to itself but it means a great deal to the creature possessing it—so much, in fact, that such a creature may not only possess it but be possessed by it.*

* Possessing a Ph.D. makes an Academian more prepossessing.

Any creature in Academe, other than a Student, that has no Ph.D. is scorned and looked down upon, being considered incompetent and incomplete. An Instructor may not have a Ph.D., but it will be trying desperately to get one. A Full Professor without a Ph.D. is an Anomaly,* unless the Full Professor is in such a field as Art, Music, or perhaps Business Administration. A President that has no Ph.D. tries to make up for it by collecting Honorary Degrees, but is always handicapped by not having what is called an Earned Doctorate.

The Ph.D., though it looms large in Academe, is actually a small creature that has a familial relationship to the Dissertation. Until it is caught by a Graduate Student, it is furtive and mouselike, hiding in crevices and behind large, dusty tomes in the Library Stacks. When pursued, it scurries off, evading capture by devious maneuvers in which it has been instructed by the Candidate's Committee.

Once it is captured, however, it begins to take on larger proportions and new significance. It will be found, unfailingly,† close behind its owner's name, and its portrait will hang in a conspicuous place on the wall of its owner's office or study. It will entitle its owner to be called "Doctor," and in some instances will cause its owner to become upset if it is not called "Doctor."

The owner of a Ph.D. is said to hold a Ph.D., although not necessarily in its hands. Such a creature may indeed be called not a Professor (i.e., Possessor) but a Ph.D., which indicates how closely identified are the owner and the owned, or the holder and the held.

A Ph.D. looks down on an M.A. and even an Ed.D. It looks up only to an M.D., since the M.D is called "Doctor"

---

* Closely related to an Aberration or a Deviation from the Norm.
† As a sign that its pursuer did not fail.

without need of any request or demand to this effect. But if an M.D. has more prestige and makes more money than a Ph.D., the two have one thing in common. Neither makes house calls.

The Phi Bete

(Aut Caesar aut nullus) *

THE Phi Bete is a species of Student, but a species that sometimes turns into a Professor. The most unusual thing about it, usually about the middle of it or wherever it is most conspicuous, is a curious key. What is so curious about the key is that it is made of gold and greatly treasured, and yet will not unlock anything. The Phi Bete, however, thinks it is the key to Knowledge, which it hopes someday to open. First, though, Knowledge must be found.†

In its incessant search for Knowledge, the Phi Bete uses its eyes and ears constantly. The result is that its eyes are encased in magnifying glasses, usually framed by tortoise

---

* Either Caesar or nothing. The Phi Bete will stop at nothing, as well as stoop to anything, to be in the Top 10 Percent. Curiously a Junior Phi Bete is superior to a Senior Phi Bete.

† The Phi Bete will often be seen fiddling with its key or, if it is a Violinist, making sure its fiddle is in key.

shells from which the tortoises have been removed. At the slightest sound, especially of Classical Music, it pricks its ears. From all this pricking, its ears are enlarged and inflamed as well as pointed upward toward the stars, the motto of the Phi Bete being *Ad astra per aspera,* or "To the stars through asparagus."

Though its ears point upward, the gaze of the Phi Bete is usually down, searching through books and Learned Journals for Knowledge. As a result, the Phi Bete is often bent double, or even triple, the latter being known as a Scholarly Bent. When it is not looking it is drinking, the Phi Bete having a Thirst for Knowledge. Where it most likes to drink is at the Pierian spring, where it often finds the Muses musing, too drunk to go back to making poetry, pottery, or whatever.

Should you be approached by a Phi Bete that has two fingers extended, do not be alarmed. This does not mean that it is a mugger, simulating a handgun, or that it is a two-fingered proctologist. It merely thinks that you also are a Phi Bete and it is preparing for the famous Phi Bete handshake, a curiously intimate entwining of the hands, usually accompanied by admiring looks—not each admiring the other but each admiring itself. They always refer to those who are not Phi Betes as *hoi polloi.**

The Phi Bete often mates with a creature that is not a Phi Bete, usually preferring it that way. Two Phi Betes together could get their keys mixed up, and besides, any Knowledge they found would have to be shared, as well as the credit for discovering it.

There is nothing wrong, however, with two Phi Betes living together in the asparagus, looking up at the stars.

---

* But never, since they know this much Greek, "the" *hoi polloi.*

The Philosopher

(Exceptis excipiendis) *

THE Philosopher, which has an owlish look, is considered the wisest creature in Academe, at least by itself. It sees no need for other subjects, since Philosophy encompasses them all. This annoys the Economists, Geologists, and others, but they try to be philosophical about it.

As in other fields, the Philosopher is inclined to specialize. It may become a Rationalist, an Empiricist, a Logical Positivist,† an Existentialist, a Phenomenologist, or no telling what else. That is, you may not be able to tell, but it will be glad to tell you. Though it has a Doctorate it also usually has a master, such as Plato, Descartes,

---

* The proper exceptions being made. Or, better, you should make exceptions for exceptional Philosophers.

† But not, if it knows what is good for it, an Illogical Positivist.

Spinoza, Locke (frequently picked and also picked over), Hume, Hegel, Kant, Nietzsche, or Heidegger. Occasionally the Philosopher will say something inscrutable, for example, "I enjoy teaching Kant," though Kant died in 1804. It also tries hard to be ethical about Ethics, logical about Logic, and stoical about the Stoics without being too skeptical about the Skeptics.*

The Philosopher believes in silent meditation but also in sound reasoning. It combines the two when it thinks out loud. It has a probing, penetrating mind. An example

* In addition it values Values and judges the value of Value Judgments.

of this is its shouting "Excelsior!" upon opening a packing case. Mostly, however, it is deep in Thought, sometimes up to its hips.

Students stand in awe of the Philosopher.* They are convinced that it thinks only Deep Thoughts. This is apparent from the way they go around shaking their heads and saying, "That's too deep for me." The less they understand the Philosopher the more they are convinced that it has a Superior Intellect, enabling it to soar to heights inaccessible to them. So it is that they continue to look up to the Philosopher, while the Philosopher looks down on them. The Philosopher, always having an axiom to grind, long ago learned that what is not understood is, *ergo,* Profound, which itself is a Profound Thought.†

The ambition of the Philosopher is to have a School of Thought bearing its name, and perhaps to become an adjective which is also a noun, such as Hegelian. Meanwhile it must be content with interpreting the interpretations of interpreters of philosophical works which require interpretation. ‡

The Philosopher has been described above as owlish. However, unlike the Great Gray Owl, or *Scotiaptex nebulosa,* which is limited to asking "Who?," the Philosopher, with far more gray matter, also asks "Why?" When it asks this of a Student, the Student is likely to ask the Philosopher "What?"

---

* They clean it off afterward.

† Somehow made more profound by the insertion of that *ergo.* See also the Latin aphorism *Sile et philosophus esto,* or "Keep silent and be counted a philosopher."

‡ The study of any philosophic work that does not require interpretation is hardly worthy of Academic Credit.

The Placement

(Sero venientibus ossa) *

THE hardest thing for the Placement to say is "I can't place you." Often it may be unable to place a Graduating Student but hates to admit it. Usually the Placement holds out Hope, holding it out as far as it can and as long as it can. Because of this it has developed Tenacity, which is something like the claw of a lobster. The Placement never relaxes, since it has no sooner placed a Student than there is another to be placed—someplace, anyplace, unless the Student is Choosy. A Choosy Student is one that has Outside Income.†

The Placement, with its Tenacity, is in touch with Busi-

---

* Those who come late get the bones. In Bad Times it is slim pickings for the Placement, no matter how early it is.

† The opposite of this is an Inside Outcome, which is something that may result from the Food Service.

ness, Industry, and the Job Market, a place where Jobs are bought and sold. From time to time representatives come from the Outside World to look at Students who display Interest. While they are On Campus, they may look at female Students who display anything interesting.

Representatives of Business and Industry set up Interviews, where they get a view of Interested Students and Interested Students get a view of them. Representatives ask such penetrating questions as "What is your Major?" and Students ask "What is your Starting Salary?" * Meanwhile the Placement is hovering nearby, still holding out Hope and perhaps praying. Every time the Placement places a Student its own place is a little securer.† The only time the Placement has mixed feelings about placing a Student is when the Student is placed in a place that pays more than the Placement is paid, and it is tempted to change places.

The Placement has a good time in Good Times and a bad time in Bad Times. Students who are not placed may think it is the fault of their Major. The Placement, however, says, "No, it is General."

The Placement keeps a Graph in its office. Its favorite Graph is one with a Rising Curve. When the President comes in, the Placement is quick to call attention to the Graph—unless it has a Declining Curve instead of a Rising Curve, in which case the Placement hides the Graph by covering it with a list of Openings ‡ or turning its face to the wall.

To keep fit, or to keep from having fits, the Placement runs in place in place of doing something someplace else.

---

* There is nothing to stop the Student from also asking about the Stopping Salary.

† The Placement is always fearful of being replaced by a Replacement.

‡ The Graph is thus, strange as it may seem, closed by Openings.

It does not like to be far from the Bulletin Board, where it puts up new Notices and takes down any Notice that is more than two years old. The Placement loves to be noticed putting up Notices, which is a sign of Activity.

The Political Scientist

(Facile omnes, quom valemus, recta consilia aegrotis damus) *

IF it were in the Outside World, the Political Scientist would be a Politician. Fortunately, however, it is in Academe, and can therefore make political decisions without fear of the consequences. It believes in government of the Political Scientists, by the Political Scientists, and for the Political Scientists, though it finds it safer to be a Consultant or a Speech Writer than an Office Holder.

Interesting as it is for the Student to study Political Science, it is more interesting to study the Political Scientist's face as it sees the Handwriting on the Wall, Foresees the Foreseeable Future, and Views with Alarm. Unlike the Historian, always looking back at the Distant Past, the Political Scientist can see the Past, the Present,

---

* When we are well, we readily give good counsel to the sick. However the Political Scientist is ready with advice no matter what its condition, and some are sick of it.

and the Future simultaneously, which accounts for a somewhat blurred vision. What it sees with the most clarity is
the Wave of the Future, though this should perhaps be
left to the Oceanographer.

The concern of the Political Scientist is Government,
and one of the courses it teaches is Comparative Government. It considers Superlative Government beyond the
grasp not only of Students of Government but of those in
the Government, unless the Government is currently in
the hands of the Party to which it subscribes.* Its favorite
course is Political Theory, which permits it to theorize,
while the course that would give it the most difficulty and
which it therefore does not offer is Political Practice, in
which day-to-day events might prove its theories wrong.

"Man," it is fond of saying, "is a political animal." A
Political Scientist rarely refers to an animal as a political
man. And though it often says that "Politics makes strange
bedfellows," it almost never cites an instance of a Hawk
lying down with a Dove. The Political Scientist frequently
refers to its Open Mind, although it does not mean by
this that its mind is empty, the contents having fallen
out while it was vigorously nodding its head in assent or
shaking its head in dissent. It is also proud of its even-
handedness, perhaps referring to both of its hands, ten
fingers being an even number, and not a single hand, with
its uneven five.

The Political Scientist often dreams of leaving Academe and going into the Outside World and Running for
Office. It keeps in shape by jogging † and, in public lectures, proving it is not easily winded. But usually it prefers
to remain in Academe, quoting such Political Thinkers as

---

* The Party to which it subscribes can be determined by the newspapers
and magazines to which it subscribes.

† Its memory.

Machiavelli, Hobbes, Locke, Coolidge, and McGovern. It thus maintains its perfect record of never having lost an election.*

The Political Scientist could obviously handle the Government better than it is being handled. But it is busy writing a textbook that it has convinced the publishers should have a substantial sale, since it will be used in all of its own classes.

Once upon a time there was a nonpartisan Political Scientist, but its courses were too dull to attract any Students. It was forced to leave Academe and cover the political scene on television. It did not last long in this profession either. The happy ending to this story is that it Espoused a Cause, marrying a woman of great wealth. This freed the former Political Scientist to abandon the projected textbook and write a potential best seller entitled *How to Get Sexual Satisfaction Out of Stuffing a Ballot Box.*

---

* Failure to be elected Most Popular Professor has nothing to do with this, since a Professor does not run for such an office, or not ostensibly.

The President

(Rex non potest peccare) *

IF there is any distinguishing feature of the President, it is its constant awareness that it is the President. One may see this in its expression, whereby it manages to say, "I am the President" without actually saying, "I am the President." It fancies itself a King or an Emperor, though both the King and the Emperor are species that are not, or not by these names, found in Academe. If the President possesses a crown, it keeps it tucked away somewhere, along with its cap and gown, and puts it on when no one is looking.

The President need not be tall, but this helps, because it is always looking over Reports and Petitions and long lists of Prospective Donors. It may even look over the

* The king can do no wrong. This is wrong, when applied to the President, but it would be wrong for anyone to say so except a Trustee.

112

walls around Academe, either to make sure they are high enough to keep out Destructive Influences or to keep in Professors who might be lured away from Academe into the Outside World, the World of Business and Politics and Making Money.

But the President itself often goes beyond the walls of Academe in search of sustenance. On these forays it is usually accompanied by the Development, which knows

how to entice and engulf such succulent morsels as the Banker, the Industrialist, and the Retired Millionaire. It is the Development also that carries the bag, or brief-case, into which such tasty tidbits are stuffed. But it is the President that disarms or unteeths such creatures of the Outside World by showing them its Degrees and perhaps distracting them by baring its Academic Credentials. It then overwhelms them with its Prestige.

Of animals, the President is a cross between the Lion, the King of the Beasts, and the Fox, known for slyness and for adeptness at getting out of Difficult Situations.* The President is especially leonine and kingly at Commence-ment, when it sits in a commanding position, as if en-throned, in its Academic Regalia.†

A curious thing about the President is that, unlike the Professor on Tenure, the President may cease being a President at any time the Trustees decree. Once it is no longer President it may be transformed, as if by magic, into a Professor, a Consultant, or an Unemployed. Some-times a President is thought to be insincere. More often, however, it is merely insecure. It rises rapidly but it may also fall rapidly. It stands on Slippery Ground.

It is said that the President sleeps at night with its eyes wide open, if indeed it sleeps at all. It may have a mate, but nonetheless it takes its Problems to bed with it. The morrow may bring Glory, and yet again it may bring Disaster.

There is no creature in Academe that has so many Fringe Benefits, but of what benefit is a benefit when it ceases to benefit? *Sic transit gloria praesidentis.*

---

* The most difficult, for the President, is a Difficult Decision.

† Commencement is a solemn occasion, closely resembling a Funeral. Wearing its doctoral hood, the President resists the impulse to wink, lest someone consider this being hoodwinked.

The Psychologist

(Quod volumus, facile credimus) *

JUST as a woodpecker pecks at a tree trunk in search of insects, the Psychologist pecks away at the Mind in search of Perception, Motivation, and Personality. Unlike the woodpecker, it does not eat such things, but the more it discovers about them the more it will be advanced, the higher its salary, and the better it will be fed. *Post hoc, ergo propter hoc,* or because of this it will not have to hock its property.

The Psychologist may be a Child Psychologist, if it is precocious, or an Abnormal Psychologist, if it is not quite normal.† Then again, if it is gregarious it may be a Social Psychologist or, if it is not quite sure that Psychology is the field it should be in, an Experimental Psychologist. One

* We readily believe what we want to believe. This is especially true if we are told by a Psychologist and it is good news.

† Some think this true of all Psychologists.

difference between a Psychologist and a Psychiatrist is that the Psychologist has a Ph.D. and the Psychiatrist has an M.D. Another difference is that the Psychologist mostly teaches, while the Psychiatrist practices, often wishing the Psychologist would practice what it teaches.

Pecking away, the Psychologist digs deeply into the Psyche, looking for Cognition, Repression, and the like but often thwarted by the Ego, Superego, and Id, as well as the Freud and the Jung. When it is not looking, the Psychologist is listening, often getting an earful of Mental Disorders.* No matter what it has an ear full of, the Psychologist is a Good Listener. One reason for this is that it can understand what is said to it but, because of Jargon, cannot be understood. Since what it says cannot be understood, what it says sounds impressive, which is why it says what cannot be understood.†

Being interested in Group Behavior, the Psychologist gets together a group of Students and takes notes on how they behave. Sometimes it asks them to describe their feelings after feeling one another. Many Students are frank and honest about this, but others merely go through the emotions. From controlled or fairly well controlled laboratory experiments in Group Behavior the following revolutionary discoveries have been made:

1. Fully 99 percent of the male and female Students in such a group feel more, or at least see more, if they are nude.

2. Under these conditions, approximately the same percentage of Students would be willing to perform the experiment again.

---

* A Mental Disorder occurs when the patient has ordered something and then, because of a change of Mind, cancels the order.

† Except by other Psychologists, or so it is understood.

3. Interestingly, the same percentage of Students would perform the experiment again and again, despite the time involved and without academic credit.*

The Psychologist often discovers instances of Maladjustment, but a little adjustment here and there, perhaps using a pipe wrench,† usually fixes things up. It is important, however, that whatever is done be Relevant.

---

* In this instance they think the credit should go to the Psychologist, especially if it enthusiastically participates in the experiment.

† One way to get a pipe smoker to stop smoking.

The R.A.

(Fide, sed cui vide) *

THE R.A., occasionally referred to as the Resident Assistant and sometimes as the Dorm Proctor, is a Student that, like the three monkeys, sees no evil, hears no evil, and speaks no evil. Or if it should see or hear any evil it says nothing to the Dean about it. Not, that is, if it knows what is good for it. If it doesn't know what is good for it, it will do what it is being given room and board to do but will be unable to sleep or eat.

The R.A. lives in a Dorm and is charged with seeing to it that Students obey the Rules. It can be not only charged but discharged, which is why it must be Circumspect. The R.A. is between the Devil and the Deep, since it needs to keep on good terms (at least two Semesters or three

---

* Trust, but take care whom you trust. If the Dean trusts the R.A. and the R.A. trusts the Students and the Students trust the R.A. and the R.A. trusts the Dean, it will be the first time in the history of Academe.

Quarters) with both the Dean and the Students.* The strain of looking up to the Dean and looking out for the Students sometimes causes the R.A. to have a Split Personality, more familiarly known as being Two-Faced. The advantage of having two faces is that it always has another face to Look the Other Way.

Some questionable activities of the Students, however, the R.A. may find it advisable to report. One is a case of assault with battery, especially when the battery has been stolen and the assault is upon the R.A. Another case is a male Student's keeping a female Student in its room overnight, while its male roommate has to sleep on the floor in the hall. The R.A. may suggest that the roommate be assigned to a Single or given a sleeping bag.†

One of the duties of the R.A. is to promote social activities in the Dorm, usually in conjunction with the Social Chairman.‡ After intensive study they may think up something novel and ingenious, such as a Beer Bust. If it is successful it may become an Annual Affair and ultimately a Tradition.

The ideal of the R.A. is an entire week in which nothing out of the Ordinary happens. The Ordinary is bad enough.

* Frequently the Dean is both the Devil and the Deep, the two rolled into one and the R.A. being the one rolled into.

† A Single is a room for one Student. A room for two Students is not a Married but a Double.

‡ A conjunction, by the way, may be coordinating, subordinating, correlative, adversative, causal, or, of special interest in connection with Dorm activities, copulative.

The Registrar

(A maximis ad minima) *

THE Registrar is usually found only in the female of the species. If there is such a thing as a male Registrar, it is almost as rare as a male Dean of Women. Often the Registrar has no mate. If it does, it may have had to go to the Outside World and search for one, taking whatever it could get. However, it may do very well without a mate, sublimating its sexual drive by pulling open drawers.

It is easy to recognize the Registrar. A quiet, harmless creature, it is covered with little black spots that, on closer inspection, turn out to be the letters *A, B, C, D, E,* and *F.* Having read *The Scarlet Letter,* the Registrar keeps the *A*'s well hidden, usually close to its heart.†

---

* From the greatest to the smallest. With the Registrar, its range of responsibilities is from minutiae to the minuscule.

† Some think the Registrar is heartless. This is not true. It may, of course, have had a heart transplant, the original heart being replaced by a computer.

The Registrar maintains the same position most of the time. This is because, unlike the Assistant Professor, there is no other position the Registrar can rise to, except out of its chair. It feeds on Rules. Along with Rules, it sometimes nibbles on Statistics. Whereas Rules are difficult to break, Statistics can be twisted at will.

The Registrar worries constantly about such things as the Calendar, Credits, Transfer, and the Examination Period. This last is closely related to the condition of Students known as the Examination Coma. One thing the Registrar enjoys is keeping Records. These it takes out and plays over and over, never seeming to tire of their haunting melodies which it alone can hear.

The daytime habitat of the Registrar is a small cave in the Administration Building. During times of stress, such as Registration, that fearful ogre, the Work Load, may force the Registrar to spend the night there. As night falls, the Registrar pulls out a drawer of the Filing Cabinet (the drawer on which there is an *R*) and curls up in a nest of papers.

Let us tiptoe away quietly and permit the Registrar to gain strength to face the tasks of the morrow. These may seem Trivia to other Academians, but they are Essential Trivia. Professors and Students are often unaware of whether the President is in its office or even On Campus. But absence of the Registrar is noted at once and is cause for alarm.

The Registrar is sometimes called "a brick," but it is more like mortar. Without this faithful creature the whole place would soon fall apart.

The Requirement

(Nec mora nec requies) *

PROBABLY the creature most hated by Students is the Requirement. The Requirement, they think, is a species closely related to the Thumbscrew and the Guillotine. It may be a Requirement in Writing, in a Foreign Language, or in Science. Or it may be a Distribution Requirement, which spreads itself over several fields and is almost impossible to get around.

The Requirement is thought by Students to be difficult, useless, and restrictive of Individual Freedom of Choice. The worst thing about the Requirement is that it is required. In fact if the Requirement were not required it might be found attractive and enjoyable. In the same

* "More necking requires more necking" is a translation unacceptable to most Latin scholars, though some may wish they had thought of it. The traditional translation is "Neither delay nor rest."

way, books on the Required Reading List might be considered delightful and inspiring if they were not on such a list or, even better, if they were on the list of Banned Books.*

To a Student, the important thing about a Requirement is discovering how to avoid it, lest it block the way to a Degree. Various devices are employed, such as a word from a Friendly Professor, a letter from a Psychiatrist, or a falsi-

* A book that is popular with Students is one that has, as it is said, got onto the Banned Wagon, or at least the *Index Expurgatorius*.

fied record. But the Requirement usually stubbornly holds its ground and grinds down the Student. It is something the Student has to go through, much like a debilitating and shattering illness. Indeed the Student may not make it, the Requirement proving fatal.*

This attitude toward the Requirement is not shared by members of the Faculty and Administration, since they believe in a Balanced Education, no matter how precariously balanced. Moreover, *they* got through the Requirement, and what was bad enough for them is bad enough for today's Students. Occasionally they give in to Student Pressure and Demands.†

The Requirement most closely resembles a ponderous pachyderm, looming large on the horizon, its wide ears flapping, its tusks gleaming in the sun, and its trunk reaching out to grab up the frightened Student. Anticipation is often worse than realization, but not in the case of the Requirement, which for a whole year holds Students in its painful grasp. The only enjoyment a Student gets out of a Requirement is, one way or another, getting out of it.

Interestingly, the Requirement in Latin has become almost extinct. This may be because of the sagacity seen, even by the Dean (*Decanus*), in the quatrain composed by an anonymous Student:

> *Amo, amas, amat,*
> *Amamus, amatis, amant.*
> That's all the Latin I know
> And all the Latin I want.

Perhaps more Students should put their ideas about the Requirement into verse.

---

* With a capital F.
† In the Old Days referred to as Requests.

The Sabbatical

(Requiescat in pace) *

THE Sabbatical is a creature that makes its appearance only once in seven years. There is no creature so much loved by the Professor, as is indicated by the impatience with which it waits through six long years to get one.

Just before it gets a Sabbatical a Professor says, "Next year I'll be on a Sabbatical." The next year, however, it says cryptically, "I'm off on a Sabbatical." To be off while being on is something understood only by Academians. Others may say of such a Professor, "He's off his rocker," but never "He's on his rocker" or "He's off on his rocker." †

A Sabbatical and a Leave-Without-Pay are as different

---

* May he (she) rest in peace. More likely the Professor on a Sabbatical is resting in Pisa.

† It is true that as soon as a Professor is on a Sabbatical it is off like a rocket.

as Day and Night, the Leave-Without-Pay being the dark, gloomy one. Nonetheless when a Professor is on a Sabbatical it takes leave of its friends and sometimes of its senses, traveling far away from its familiar haunts, even though they may still haunt it.* In letters home it makes such strange remarks about its activities as "I am holed up in a pension on the Left Bank." It should be explained for Non-Academians that the Professor on a Sabbatical has not been held up, a pension in this instance is not something one gets after retirement, and the Left Bank is not an ultraliberal financial institution.†

When a Professor is off on a Sabbatical it usually says it is "working on a book." It does this in a library, where there are plenty of books to work on. Meanwhile the Librarian watches nervously, often thinking the book is one that does not need working on and being prepared to intercede if the Professor slips under the covers or starts gluing together pages.

When the Sabbatical the Professor is on is over,‡ the Professor returns to Academe. It wants its Colleagues to take note of the notes it has taken, assuring them it had permission to take them and will eventually return them to their owner.§ Actually the Professor hopes to make the notes into a book, which is a little like turning lead into gold. More likely, however, the notes will remain notes and will be filed away until Spring Recess, Summer Vaca-

---

* As Thomas Haynes Bayly almost said, "A Leave of Absence makes the heart grow fonder."

† The above does not say what the Professor said but what it did not say, which is known by the Philosopher as Negative Positivism.

‡ Another confusing concept.

§ The Professor takes its notes with a pen, but others take them *cum grano salis,* i.e., with a grain of salt, which must be difficult to dip into an inkwell.

tion, or the next Sabbatical, after which they will be filed away again or left for Posterity.

It should be noted that the Professor on a Sabbatical is never spoken of as a Dropout, a term that is reserved for Students, or even, being *on* a Sabbatical, a Dropoff. Nevertheless for a semester (full pay) or a year (half pay) the Professor in many ways resembles a Dropout. It too leaves Academe. It too drops its responsibilities. And it too may even drop out of sight. Unlike the Student Dropout, however, it drops its friends a card now and then, telling what it is doing or what it is supposed to be doing.

Sometimes the Sabbatical is joined by a Fellowship or a Grant. The Professor that is off on both a Sabbatical and a Fellowship or a Grant goes around with a broad grin *
and an enlarged *curriculum vitae*.

* Better than a narrow grin and much like a smug smile.

The Scholarship

(Pecuniae obediunt omnia) *

IF the Scholarship is not a ship, neither is every Student a Scholar. However, the Scholarship is a buoyant creature that keeps many a Student afloat. It might be compared to a friendly cetacean, perhaps a purposeful porpoise. The Student that fails to get a Scholarship says, grimly, "I'm sunk."

The Scholarship is of the same genus as the Financial Aid (which is something like a Band-Aid), except that the Scholarship does not expect to be paid back, and therefore is never disappointed in its expectations. The Scholarship provides the Student with support, not only where it needs it but, more important, when it needs it. But for the Scholarship, the Student might never have been admitted

* All things yield to money. A Student on a Scholarship finds doors opening all over Academe.

to Academe. Also but for the Scholarship, the Student might have had to leave Academe and go to work, doing something useful and productive. To such a Student, the Outside World is known not as the Outside World but as the Cruel World, its particular brand of cruelty being that it expects the Student to pay its own way and to support itself instead of being supported by a Scholarship.

There are at least two species of Scholarship, but they have the same end.* One is the State Scholarship, paid by

* Curiously, they have only one end, and this is to support the Student. It must be the lower end.

the taxpayer. The other is the Name Scholarship. The Name Scholarship has the Donor's name on it, whereas the State Scholarship does not have the taxpayer's name on it. The difference between a Donor and a Taxpayer is that a Donor cannot be jailed for not donating. The Donor gives a Scholarship either (1) to perpetuate its name, (2) out of School Spirit, or (3) as a Tax Deduction. There are no strings attached, except that the Student on a Name Scholarship be of Good Christian Character, while the Student on a State Scholarship be In Need.

The Scholarship scorns the wealthy. This is why it is difficult to find a Student that has wealthy parents, at least at the time of application for a Scholarship. Parents just back from a Mediterranean cruise suddenly become Poverty Stricken. Some go on Relief, eating nothing but food stamps, until their son or daughter gets a Scholarship, whereupon they start driving their Cadillac in public again. Not having to pay Room, Board, and Tuition is Relief enough, and they are grateful to the helpful Scholarship for not having to give up their maid and butler.

A Scholarship may, of course, be the result of competition, the Student winning a Scholarship having the highest College Board Scores, being in the top Percentile, and being either the president of the student body or the captain of the football team. The Scholarship may be embarrassed, however, if the Student it supports turns out to excel also in such extracurricular activities as cheating, thieving, and drug pushing, along with occasional arson and rape. Such misdemeanors may draw a rebuke from the Student Council and even loss of the Scholarship.*

Loss of a Scholarship is a little like loss of virginity, and it means more to some than to others.

---

* The Scholarship is not really lost, only to the Student.

The Scientist

(Res non posse creari de nilo) *

THERE are two major types of Scientist, the Pure Scientist and the Applied (and presumably Impure) Scientist. The Pure Scientist must not think any bad thoughts or have any naughty ideas, because these are made into Rules which the Applied Scientist has to carry out.† The Scientist uses what is called the Scientific Method, experimenting, collecting data, and finally making a Generalization or a Scientific Law. For instance the Scientist may jump out of a window again and again until it proves that falling bodies fall until they hit some solid object, such as the ground. The Scientist is known for Perseverance.

* Matter cannot be created from nothing. Discovery of this astonishing fact was a great breakthrough for the Scientist. It came about in answer to the question, "What is the matter?"

† It carries them out of Academe and leaves them with Industry and others to dispose of.

Scientists are not all alike. For instance there is the Physicist. But for the Physicist there would have been no such inventions as the electric light, the short circuit, and electrocution; the telephone, the wrong number, and the busy signal; the automobile, traffic accidents, and air pollution. It is to the Physicist that we owe the X ray, the X-rated movie,* and the "*X* marks the spot" where a city was before the nuclear bomb was dropped.

As for the Chemist, when it is not away delivering papers † it is usually poring over formulas or pouring into test tubes. It does not actually test tubes but the chemicals it pours into them. Through its analysis of Quantitative Analysis and Qualitative Analysis it has learned how to change one thing into another. For instance it knows how to change a tree into paper, though it is still working on a chemical formula for changing paper into a living, growing tree.‡

The Chemist can change just about anything into something else, making solids into gases, coal into electricity, and soybeans into plastics. Iron, it should be noted, changes into rust without any help. Because it has to handle so many things when in the Lab, such as test tubes, flasks, beakers, and Bunsen burners (used for burning Bunsens), and because it gets into just about everything, including trouble if it mixes the wrong chemicals and causes an explosion,§ the Chemist is or should be akin to an octopus. If you ask any Chemist, it will tell you it has its hands full.

The Scientist may also be a Biologist, concentrating on

---

* Or any movie, including movies that are good morally and bad in every other way.

† At Conferences and Symposiums held in pleasant places to which travel is tax-deductible.

‡ Many hope it will not succeed, since Academians already find it difficult to see the forests because of the trees.

§ The only thing more dangerous, in Academe, is mixing metaphors.

such things as organs, organisms, and orgasms. The first two it looks at through a microscope. The Biologist teaches Students the difference between blood cells and prison cells and insists that heredity can be more than just inheriting money.*

While the Biologist is interested only in living things, the Geologist concentrates on rocks, which have been dead as long as anyone can remember. In fact the Geologist tells Students exactly how many billion years old the Earth is, and the Students, though unconvinced, dutifully write this down. Nothing, they believe, could be that old, not even the Geology Professor.

Sociologists think they too are Scientists, and often refer to themselves as Social Scientists. So also Political Scientists, Military Scientists, and Christian Scientists. But you have to draw the line somewhere. In Academe, according to Conservative Trustees,† the line forms on the left.‡

---

* There is also the Marine Biologist, from the halls of Montezuma to the shores of Tripoli.

† Are there any others?

‡ No mention has been made of those honest-to-goodness and sometimes honest-to-badness Scientists, the Zoologists, the Botanists, and the Astronomers. But the word "science" comes from the Latin *scire,* to know, and to know everything would make one a know-it-all, which one would not wish to be called.

The Semester and the Quarter

(Tempus fidget)

THE Semester and the Quarter are the Odd Couple of Academe, but they are never found together. In some parts of Academe the Semester is, as they say, "adopted." Apparently it is hard for Academians to give birth to such a creature, but they take it under their wing.* Before they take it under their wing they take it under advisement during a period somewhat longer than gestation.

The Semester is longer than the Quarter, and it gives Professors a better chance to "get close" to their Students. Sometimes they even "get in contact" with them, in this instance getting close indeed, and if the Professor and the Student are of opposite sexes this can lead to Ugly Rumors.

Literally a Semester is half a year or six months (the

* All Academians do not have wings, though they may soar on flights of fancy.

Latin *sex,* six, plus *mensis,* month). But since the Academic
Year is only nine months, to allow Students three months
to forget what they have learned, the Semester is half of
nine months, less Registration, Vacations, Recesses, etc.,
or about sixteen weeks.

Still, it is longer than the Quarter, which is a third of
nine months, less Registration, Vacation, Recesses, etc. A
Quarter is just long enough for a Professor to learn the
names of the Students in a class, if it is a small class, and
at the end of the Quarter to make some such memorable
remark as "Time flies." *

There is strong feeling in Academe about the Semester
and the Quarter. Some Administrators and Professors
prefer one and some prefer the other. The struggle at times
becomes bitter. "No Quarter!" cry those who believe in
the Semester. Students generally favor the Quarter, knowing that after subtracting time spent in the first days and
weeks assigning texts, distributing syllabuses,† etc. and in
the last days and weeks explaining earlier explanations,
there is little time left for study and tests. In what is called
Year-Around Operation, there are four Quarters in the
Year, just as there are four quarters in a dollar. But most
Students and Professors find three Quarters of the Academic variety a sufficient drain on the Intellect.

Earlier it was pointed out that the Semester derives from
the Latin *sex* plus *mensis.* This is not to say there is no sex
in the Quarter, though unless there is what is known as the
speedup, with more class meetings,‡ there obviously cannot be quite so much.

The advantages and disadvantages of the Semester and

---

* It requires a steady hand, fast reflexes, and a stopwatch.
† Or, if you are opposed to busing, syllabi.
‡ Both high class and low class.

the Quarter are not understood in the Outside World. Nor are they, if truth be told, in Academe. However there is a Committee "looking into the matter." Constantly looking into this matter and other matters undoubtedly causes eyestrain and is probably why so many Academians wear glasses. Reading Student handwriting in Examinations * could, however, be a contributing factor.

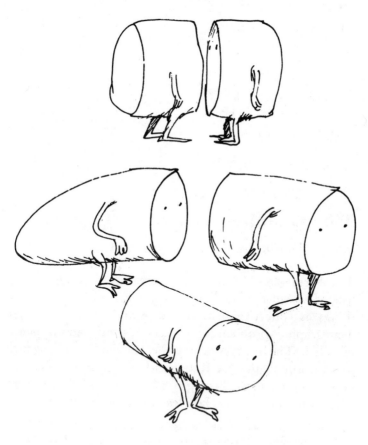

* And sometimes in hieroglyphics. The Rosetta stone has proved useful.

The Sociologist

(Homo homini aut deus aut lupus) *

THE Sociologist is a many-sided creature. It is also many-faceted or, since it is inclined to run on and on about such things as collective behavior, race and ethnic relations, demographic problems, and social stratification, many-fauceted. The many sides of the Sociologist rub against the Anthropologist, the Religionist, the Criminologist, the Educationist, and the Ecologist, as well as other Sociologists. All of this rubbing can be pleasant enough, especially be-

---

* Man is either a god or a wolf toward his fellow man. The Sociologist might accept such middle-of-the-road alternatives as a demigod, a fox, or a snake. The word "demigod," by the way, reminds one of *demivierge,* the French term for a half-virgin or a virgin whose sexual activities stop short of intercourse. This should interest a Sociologist.

tween males and females of its own or related species, but it can also cause friction.

The Sociologist has many concerns, even when it is not an Industrial Sociologist, with business concerns paying a Consultant's fee and not being quite sure whether what is needed is an Industrial Sociologist or an industrious Chairman of the Board. Mainly, however, the Sociologist is concerned about people living together, and this has nothing to do with whether they are married or Living in Sin, so long as they are sincere about it. The Sociologist is less interested in the individual than in watching what people do in a group or what it calls a societal segment, and therefore is always taking a close look at their private activities. Thus the Sociologist may often be identified by its carrying binoculars, a pen, and a scratch pad.*

Social behavior fascinates the Sociologist, as also such social misbehavior as juvenile delinquency and crime. The Sociologist is seldom sent to prison but often takes a class into one on a field trip, especially if the field is criminology. The considerate and thoughtful Sociologist will always count its Students before and after visiting a prison. If there are either more or fewer as the class departs, it surmises that something is amiss.†

The Sociologist also delves into such matters as the Family, and whether it is better to live in the old-fashioned familial relationship or in an up-to-date Commune. It carefully explains to Students the difficulty of obtaining a divorce without first being married, and if interested in making use of visual aids may put on a fashion show, displaying the latest in paternity suits. Speaking of divorce, one finds it difficult to divorce Mathematics from Sociology, since the Sociologist is concerned about how many children the average family may have and still maintain Zero Population Growth.‡

All in all, the Sociologist is one of the busiest creatures in Academe. Though society is its specialty, it may have to avoid society in order to work on a paper on social problems.

---

* Always helpful if the Sociologist should develop an itch.

† Or added.

‡ The Sociologist itself may have five or six children, which will require someone to have fewer than no children to even out.

The Tenure

(Salvus) *

THE Tenure is constantly being sought by Instructors and Assistant Professors. To those who seek it, it is an elusive, tantalizing creature, always keeping its distance and beckoning as if to say, "Keep coming" (i.e., coming forth with publications) and "Just a little more." Some who never reach it think it is a Phantom or a Mirage, luring them ever onward and upward and then vanishing at the final Evaluation.

But those who reach it, such as the Associate Professor and the Full Professor, find it something to cling to or something that clings to them. As the years go by, it winds itself around them like a vine, protecting them from the slings and arrows of outraged Administrators, Colleagues, and Trustees. The Tenure also resembles a shell, into

* Safe. Once a Professor gains Tenure it also gains Stature, but above all it is Secure.

which the Academian occupant can withdraw like a turtle or a crab, snug and safe until Retirement.

Though the Tenure does not inhibit the creature that has at last achieved it, it sharply decreases the inclination to move from place to place. In some instances the grip of the tentacles of Tenure is so firm that the mind, if not the body, of the Tenured Academian is stationary. Having reached Tenure, or having been reached and held securely by Tenure, why should it continue to struggle?

There is a gluey quality about the Tenure. This may be a discharge, although Discharge is the very thing it protects against. At any rate this substance quickly hardens, thereby adding to the protective encasement of the Academian within.

The comforting grip of the Tenure may be relaxed, however, if the Trustee has its way. Indeed the Tenure may be uprooted, or killed off by a spray of Withering Remarks and Rigorous Resolutions, and banished from Academe forever. The Trustee especially is "out to get" the Tenure, but, curiously, if it were actually to get the Tenure itself, it might find it not such a bad thing after all.

It makes a great deal of difference who has the Tenure, just as it makes a great deal of difference who has the Common Cold. However, the Tenure, unlike the Common Cold, is hard to catch.*

---

* Increasingly, the Tenure is becoming tenuous. A Tenured Professor may be removed for Cause, but the Cause must be something terribly bad, bad enough to be frowned upon even by the AAUP and the ACLU.

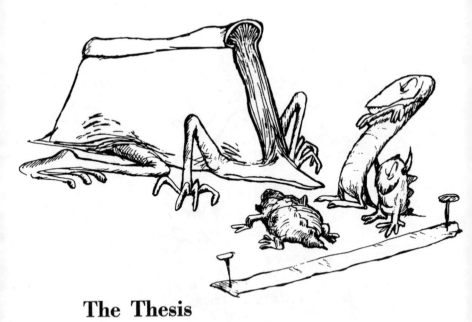

The Thesis

(Totidem verbis) *

PERHAPS because it realizes it is smaller than the Dissertation and has fewer notes on its feet, or footnotes, the Thesis tries to look larger and more important than it really is. While its hide is of stiff, heavy material, its insides are white and as thick as possible. Its insides are not pure white, however, only its margins, which are abnormally wide. In the very center of each of its inner parts, surrounded by these wide margins, are black letters in pica type. It would seem more distinguished † to have the type known as elite, but pica has the advantage of taking up more space.

The Thesis is rectangular in shape and despite all of its efforts to fatten up is usually rather thin. The most im-

* In just so many words. What really counts, in a Thesis, is the number of words, or pages, and these are carefully counted.

† Though slightly less distinguishable.

portant part of the Thesis is the number on its rear end. The higher the number,* the more pleased the Thesis is with itself.

Also important in connection with the Thesis is its Deadline. When it is born or, even earlier, when it is conceived, the Deadline is already on its mind. As time goes on, it becomes more and more worried about its Deadline and may die of concern and foreboding. Its fate is so inextricably connected with its Deadline that it has no chance of survival if the Deadline expires first.

Holding the Thesis back, when it is trying desperately to reach its Deadline, are all manner of malicious little creatures. These include Disapprovals, Revisions, and Charges of Plagiarism. They continually get in the way of the Thesis, obstructing its progress and frustrating its attempts to pass. "Let me pass," begs the Thesis, but it gets nothing but derisive laughter and seems doomed to fail.

The Thesis is often said to be going forward when it is at a standstill or, if it is not yet on its feet, a sitstill. Frequently it is gathering dust, though it tells everyone it is gathering facts. There is something snail-like about the Thesis, though the snail's pace is considerably faster.

The Thesis remains in embryonic form longer than most creatures of Academe, except of course the Dissertation. Sometimes it remains in this form until the Deadline has come and gone. The Deadline never comes again, one look at the still unformed Thesis apparently being enough.

The Thesis is born of Necessity. The other parent is unknown, wisely deciding to remain anonymous.

In many ways the Thesis is the most pathetic creature in Academe, even if it grows to full stature, reaches its Deadline, and passes. It is not a mountain made out of a molehill but a molehill made out of a mountain.†

* Which does not mean higher up on its end.
† Or what seems to have been a mountain of labor.

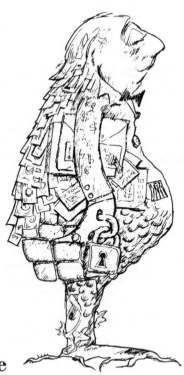

The Trustee

(Aut doce aut disce aut discede) *

IF you look closely you will see that the Trustee has a green back. In fact if you look even more closely you will see that its back is covered with greenbacks. Other creatures, such as the President and the Development, are always rubbing up against the Trustee and patting it on the back, hoping some of the green stuff will come off.

The Trustee leads a double life. When it visits Academe, which is once or twice a year, it is a Trustee. The rest of the time it is some such thing as a Banker or a Lawyer or a Stockbroker or a Conservative. It is never a Truck Driver or a Street Sweeper or a Clerk. In the Outside World it has standing, but in Academe it sits on the Board.†

---

* Teach, learn, or leave. That is what the Trustee would like to tell Professors and Students.

† It also sits on, and quashes, Impractical Ideas.

The Trustee has piercing eyes when looking at the Budget or at the publications of a Leftist Professor. Otherwise, especially at a meeting of Trustees, its eyes are closed. Frequently its mind is also, though it is hard to tell unless you hear it say something. Its eyes open quickly, however, when mention is made of one of its deadly enemies, such as the Deficit or the Tenure or the Sabbatical.

A way to distinguish the Trustee from other creatures in Academe is its sleek, well-fed look. The Trustee often has a pot, which is where its stomach should be, and its hair is recently barbered and well brushed. The color of its hair is usually white, which indicates that the Trustee is of a species related to Age and Experience. These in turn are related to Judgment and Wisdom. The Trustee is proud of its breeding, though it may be thought too old for this sort of thing.

By one of the odd quirks of Academe, when it is thought to be near death it is made a Life Trustee. As such, it is not permitted to cast a vote, the strain of throwing even a small piece of paper being considered too much for it.*

---

* It is all right, though, for it to throw its money away, as long as it is thrown in the direction of the Development.

The Tuition

(Absque argento omnia vana) *

ONE seldom mentions the Tuition without also mentioning its close friends and constant companions, Room and Board. The only time the three are not found together is when a Student lives Off Campus and then is concerned only with the Tuition. The name of the Tuition comes from the Latin verb *tueri, tuitus, tutus,* to watch, guard, protect. Thus in a sense, and sometimes innocence, it is money paid by the Student's parents to see that the Student is kept out of trouble, or put away, for a period of four years.†

* Without money all efforts are in vain. Higher education keeps getting higher, but it is still possible for the rich to get a poor education.

† It may be only a coincidence that the term "term" is used both in Academe and in prison.

But the Tuition is also related to the Tutor, so that the Tuition has, or should have, something to do with teaching or being taught. However, when a Student says it "pays Tuition," it does not really pay the Tuition. It pays the Business Office, which in turn pays the Administration,

the Faculty, the Grounds Force, and the Incidental Expenses. What it pays, as the Student is repeatedly told, and told again * when it becomes an Alum, is not enough to cover everything. The difference is made up by the Endowment, and a well-endowed college is very nearly as attractive as well-endowed Co-Ed.

As the Tuition grows larger and larger, its increase in size is announced in smaller and smaller type. The Incoming Student is also informed that the Tuition does not include Fees, which are small creatures that cling to the Tuition and try to escape notice. These are given such names as the Health Fee, the Lab Fee, the Late Registration Fee, and, for those that cannot be broken of the habit of playing the organ, the Practice Fee.

The Tuition can be paid in a Lump Sum, which may explain its lumpy appearance, or in Installments. Unlike empty bottles, the Tuition is not returnable, whether the Student returns or not.

The opposite of the Tuition is the Intuition. Unlike the Tuition, the Intuition is free. It comes as standard equipment with the brain, and is not an extra. Intuition is knowing something immediately, without being taught, and if it were more prevalent would mean a drastic change in Academe: Professors would no longer be necessary. Nor, in fact, would Academe. Also, since everything would be seen with the mind's eye, on which it would be difficult to fit glasses, ophthalmologists, optometrists, and opticians would be unnecessary.

Until Intuition becomes more evident, it is probably unnecessary to say that the Tuition is necessary.† Tuition is essential in Academe, the land of the Fee.

---

* And again.

† Except in a State Institution. There is no Tuition in an Insane Asylum.

Inconclusive Conclusion

AND SO, reluctantly, we leave the Strange Land of Academe and the even stranger creatures that inhabit it. It has been a brief and partial, if not impartial, visit. Many fascinating features and creatures have been left unmentioned, largely on purpose.

The Land of Academe is unique. It is as different from the Outside World as the Outside World is different from the Land of Academe, which is an Astute Observation. If it is not the best of all possible worlds, neither is is the worst.* What makes the Land of Academe so remarkable is that it is the best of all *impossible* worlds. It is therefore probably best to make the best of it.†

* This, admittedly, is hairsplitting, something done with such frequence and precision in Academe that it has become a Fine Art.

† With reference to "impossible worlds," above, a typographical error, which may not have been an error at that, first had this as "impossible words." Academe is, after all, the land of *sesquipedalia verba,* or words that are too long to be understood by anyone but an Academian.